REFLECTIONS ON THE
TEACHINGS OF
MAHARISHI

A Personal Journey

John C. Hornburg

1ˢᵗ WORLD
PUBLISHING

REFLECTIONS ON THE TEACHINGS OF MAHARISHI
A Personal Journey

John C. Hornburg

Published by 1st World Publishing
P.O. Box 2211, Fairfield, Iowa 52556
tel: 641-209-5000 • fax: 866-440-5234
web: www.1stworldpublishing.com

First Edition

LCCN: 2014910725
SoftCover ISBN: 978-1-59540-859-4
HardCover ISBN: 978-1-59540-860-0
eBook ISBN: 978-1-59540-960-7

For Tom Egenes,
My long-time friend and teacher

An Indian Parable

There are two goddesses alive in the human breast. Lakshmi is the bestower of wealth and prosperity, and Saraswati is the giver of knowledge. Lakshmi is a very jealous goddess—if she finds out you're following Saraswati, she chases you with her riches.

There is nothing in this book that one must *do*. No advice is given and there are no rules to follow. Where certain actions would ordinarily be advised for self-improvement, the emphasis is on how the human organism heals itself through self-awareness. This awareness is both on the level of ordinary day-to-day consciousness—where we are aware of our short-comings—and ultimately on the level of Absolute Pure Consciousness, the source and healer of all things. Nature knows how to heal the organism it created, and the ability of self-knowledge it placed within us is the activating factor. This is the simple ability we all have to *see* and *know*. I give you what I have learned from Maharishi only to help you see. For from seeing develops knowing, and knowing accomplishes everything.

CONTENTS

Introduction to
His Holiness Maharishi Mahesh Yogi
and the Shankara Tradition

When Maharishi came out of the Himalayas in 1955 to teach Transcendental Meditation he said that there is no obstacle to unity with God and yet everywhere man is suffering. One is reminded of Rousseau's first words in the *Social Contract* written two hundred years earlier: Man is born free and everywhere he is in chains.

In his commentary to Ch. 2, v. 40 of the *Bhagavad-Gita* Maharishi explains that there is no obstacle to Self-realization as long as spiritual meditation is designed to take advantage of the mind's *natural tendency* to seek a field of greater happiness: "As water flows down a slope in a natural way, so the mind flows in the direction of bliss." Since the mind flows naturally toward the ocean of bliss within, it is obvious that attempts to control the mind in meditation can only impede the process. Spiritual life has been thought difficult, Maharishi says, only because of a misguided philosophy of controlling the mind "which has persisted for many centuries."

Maharishi Mahesh Yogi, a life celebate, was born Mahesh Prasad Varma in Raipur, central India, on Jan. 12, 1917 and passed into *mahasamadhi* (a Yogi's final conscious exit from the body) on Feb. 5, 2008. Because the manuscript was close to completion at the time of his passing, I have not changed anything. And anyway Maharishi is still very much in the present tense. Indeed, some experience a choser walk with him than before. The word "Maharishi" (MaHArishi) comes from the Sanskrit *maha* (great) and *rishi* (seer). A rishi is one who sees the Truth; a maharishi is one who enlivens Truth in the lives of others. "Mahesh" refers to Shiva, a member of the Hindu sacred triad (or Trinity), whom Maharishi often speaks of as a Natural Law, the force responsible for the destruction of ignorance in the world. When people started calling him Maharishi, he said, "I accepted it. Otherwise I must think of something else for them to call me."

Maharishi has been teaching around the world since 1955. Now living and working in Holland, he has revived several of the forty systems of Vedic literature. Maharishi Transcendental Meditation® is a revival of the system of *Vedanta*. From the Sanskrit roots *Veda* (knowledge) and *anta* (end), Vedanta means the culmination of knowledge in the perfect unity of man with God, Nature, and himself.

Generally not much is known about the lives of saints. But in his lectures over the years Maharishi has brought out bits and pieces of his life in terms of the 54-year history of his Transcendental Meditation movement. In my more-than-40-year association with him and his teachings I have been privileged to hear many of these discussions, both in person and on tape.

I rarely wrote anything down; his words enliven truths at the deepest level of the mind and establish themselves permanently. Therefore, even though there are no extant references to cite for many of his verbal statements, I use quotation marks throughout the book to exphasize the directness with which they struck me and the immediacy with which I still remember them—having brought them to mind many times over the years. Some of the quotes may not be exactly accurate, but they are all true.

With him I often felt like the apostles must have felt at

the feet of Christ. One cannot know what it means to be in the presence of such a perfect master. By his unity with *Brahm* (Brahman, Totality) he can speak only the truth, and over time his words structure an oracle in consciousness to which any question may be referred. His pronouncements have the authority of commands of God and, as consciousness evolves, can create knowledge and rectify behavior as soon as they are heard. And above all there is the trust factor: In this confusing world it is an incomparable comfort to be able to accept someone implicitly and wholly for what he is reputed to be, so that you are freed sink deeply into his words and divine the great Truths that rest there. This is the meeting-point of universal Truth and human intelligence.

Maharishi owns a Bachelor's degree in physics from Allahabad University, where he is said to have been a member of the swimming team. One evening a friend took him to see a wise man who lived in a little hut on the edge of the forest. It was dark inside except for a candle burning on a low table. Several disciples sat at the man's feet. Maharishi didn't see the man's face except in the headlights of a car that occasionally passed on the nearby road, but at the end of the evening he asked to be accepted as a disciple. The man was called Swami Brahmananda Saraswati and would later be referred to by everyone in the Transcendental Meditation movement simply as *Guru Dev* (the divine teacher). That evening, however, he advised that the young man finish his studies first.

Swami Brahmananda (the "bliss of Brahm") entered mahasamadi in 1953 at age 85. He was also a life celibate. Born into a wealthy family, he left home at age nine to become a *sanyasi*, renouncing worldly life to seek liberation in God consciousness. One day when he was still new to the renunciate's life, he stopped at a forest hut to ask for some fire. Sanyasis vow not to use fire to cook food; they carry a bowl and are often given food by religious people seeking merit. A man, also a sanyasi, came to the door. When asked for fire he exploded in anger and shouted, "There is no fire here!" In his innocence, the nine-year-old revealed the true meaning of the renunciation of fire by his reply: "If there is no fire here, then what is this flaring up?"

Some years later Guru Dev found his own master. Soon he was sent to a cave in the forest to meditate for long hours in solitude. After some time the master dispatched another disciple from the ashram to arrange for him to stay a few days with his student. Guru Dev must have said that the cave was already full, because the messenger returned very upset. When he reported that he had been told there was no room in the cave, the master smiled in understanding of his disciple's growing awareness of Self; the cave was full of himself. Maharishi said, "That was when every disciple in the ashram went flat on his face in reverence for Guru Dev's attainment." Guru Dev achieved Self-realization when he was still in his teens.

In the Introduction to *Maharishi Mahesh Yogi on the Bhagavad-Gita: A New Translation and Commentary, Chs. 1-6,* Maharishi wrote about the loss of the Supreme Knowledge over time and the revivals by Krishna, Buddha, Shankara, and Swami Brahmananda Saraswati. Each revival has been based on restoration of Being (pure Existence, the Absolute) as the basis of thought and action. For 2,500 years, he says, the core message of all teachers of the Shankara tradition has been the necessity of inculcating Absolute Being (Brahm) in one's awareness as the basis of life in accordance with Natural Law, which brings man out of suffering. Creation is permeated by the bliss of the Creator. "As a mountain of snow is nothing but water," Maharishi says, "this whole universe is nothing but bliss." The *Taittiriya Upanishad* declares, "Out of bliss these beings are born; in bliss they are sustained, and to bliss they go and merge again."

About 5,000 years ago Lord Krishna brought Being to light as the basis of life, and taught it as the foundation of all thinking, which in turn is the basis of all doing. Two thousand years after Krishna's revival, when the knowledge had again been lost "through the long lapse of time," Buddha came with the same essential message. Maharishi writes in his commentary on the *Bhagavad-Gita*,

> He advocated meditation in order to purify the field of thought through direct contact with Being....[His] message was complete because He incorporated the fields of Being, thinking and doing in His theme of revival. But because his followers failed to correlate these different fields of life in a systematic matter...realization of Being as the basis of a good life became obscured....the effect was mistaken for the cause. [That is] Right action came to be regarded as a means to gain nirvana, whereas right action is in fact the result of this state of consciousness in freedom.

Three or four hundred years after Buddha (about 600 B.C.E.) the master Shankara (SHANkara) again revived the ancient wisdom. Time is a factor in the loss of knowledge, Maharishi says, but also the difference in the level of consciousness between the teacher and the taught. "It has been the misfortune of every teacher that, while he speaks from his level of consciousness, his followers can only receive his message on their level; and the gulf between the teaching and understanding grows wider with time."

Shankara was as great a master as Krishna, Buddha, Christ, Mohammed and other founders of great religions, but was fated to remain out of the public eye. He was born to do a certain important thing—as we all are, if we could just discover what it is—and that was to revive the Supreme Knowledge at a time when, like today, negativity in civilization had reached critical mass.

> Shankara restored the wisdom of the Absolute [Maharishi continues] and established It in the daily life of the people, strengthening the fields of thought and action by the power

of Being....[He] not only revived the wisdom of integrated life and made it popular in his day, but also established four principal seats of learning in the four corners of India to keep his teaching pure and to ensure that it would be propagated in its entirely generation after generation. For many centuries his teaching remained alive in his followers, who lived the ideal state of knowledge with devotion. But in spite of all his fore-sight and endeavors, Shankara's message inevitably suffered... the same misfortunes as those of the other great teachers.

If the occupants of a house forget the foundations, it is because the foundations lie underground, hidden from view. It is no surprise that Being was lost to view, for It lies in the transcendental field of life.

(All succeeding directors of Shankara's four seats of learning are called by the term Shankaracharya, meaning "teacher in the tradition of Shankara." Maharishi says this is why modern scholars sometimes mistakenly place the original Shankara as late as 800 C.E.)

Shankara had disciples by the time he reached his late teens. The atmosphere around him was charged with the waves of wisdom that arose from conversations with his disciples. One of the disciples, Trotaka, seldom participated in these discussions. He preferred to appreciate his master on the level of love and service. He devoted himself to mundane tasks such as cleaning, cooking and washing clothes, so Shankara would have time for more important things. Often a group of disciples would sit on the banks of a nearby river going over points of Vedic knowl-edge while Trotaka washed his master's clothes. Legend has it that one day Shankara and the disciples assembled to return to the ashram and forgot about Trotaka. As they reached the ashram (the monastery of *Jyotir Math*) one of them looked back, and here came Trotaka moving along slowly carrying Shankara's clothes and joyously singing in a tuneful voice.

In a publication for teachers of Transcendental Medita-tion, Maharishi wrote that Trotaka's song in praise of his guru thrilled the air and purified the whole valley of the monastery. It was sweet and richly harmonious, sung in a previously unheard and unknown metre...in words overflowing with wisdom and heart-melting melody. He had gained Enlightenment and a most refined state of intellect through the instrumentality of his love for his master and his master's love for him.

Trotaka's Enlightenment fulfilled the law that perfected love inevitably becomes perfect knowledge. (The reverse is not true.) That Trotaka's song broke through the time-honored boundries of Vedic meter suggests the uniqueness of his realization. In the end Shankara placed Trotaka in charge of the monastery of Jyotir Math, making him the first exponent of the Shankaracharya tradition of knowledge in Northern India.

At the ripe old age of twenty Shankara journeyed from the Himalayas to Banaras (now Varanasi) to convince the Vedic elders of the two fundamental truths of his revival: *Atma* is Brahm and *sattva* is not Atma. These are the two essential truths at the highest level of the spiritual life. Atma—the Self, Absolute Being, the infinite, eternal Pure Consciousness experienced in meditation transcendental to thought and the phenomenal world—is essentially the same as Brahm, which is the daily-life experience of the manifest universe as essentially nothing but pure Being (the Self, Atma). This is the essence of Shankara's *Advaita* Vedanta. Advaita means non-dual: the Self and the world are one, and the same thing. Practically speaking, this means that once one has learned the technique to experience the transcendental Self, there is nothing more to be done for full Enlightenment except regular practice, understanding of one's experiences, and unstrained activity during the day. But just as important for the seeker of total Self-realization, sattva is not Atma: Sattva—the bliss-filled thoughts at the subtlest level of the thinking mind—are not yet the transcendental Atma. This means that regardless of the purity of one's life, his high birth, his development through other spiritual practices, etc. if transcending is missing one falls short of the full potential of human life.

In 1941, after many attempts over twenty years, Guru Dev was finally persuaded to leave the forest and become Shankaracharya of Northern India. The position had been vacant for 150 years for lack of an individual of sufficient realization. "In his 60 years in the forest," Maharishi has said, "he cultivated a light that will shine for 10,000 years." Maharishi wrote to his teachers:

> For the greater part of his life [Guru Dev] lived in quiet, lonely places, the habitats of lions and leopards, in hidden caves and thick forests, where even the mid-day sun frets and fumes in vain to dispel the darkness that may be said to have made a permanent abode in those solitary and distant… mountain ranges.
>
> His entire personality exhaled always the serene perfume of spirituality. His face radiated that rare light which comprises love, authority, serenity and self-assuredness; the state that comes only by righteous living and divine realization. His *darshan* [formal viewing of the person of a saint] made the people feel as if some ancient Maharishi of Upanishadic fame had assumed human form again, and that it is worthwhile leading a good life and to strive for realization of the Divine.

This is how Maharishi's presence effects those around him. To be in the presence of someone like this is to know that Self-realization needs no further proof.

In his Preface to the *Bhagavad Gita* Maharishi wrote:

> This age has…been fortunate. It has witnessed the living example of a man inspired by Vedic wisdom in its wholeness and thus able to revive the philosophy of the integrated life in all its truth and fullness. His Divinity Swami Brahmananda Saraswati, the inspiration and guiding light of this commentary on the *Bhagavad-Gita*, adorned the seat of Shankaracharya

of the North and, glowing in divine radiance, embodied in himself the head and heart of Shankara. He expounded the Truth in Its all-embracing nature. His quiet words, coming from the unbounded love of his heart, pierced the hearts of all who heard him and brought enlightenment to their minds. His message was the message of fullness of heart and mind. He moved as the living embodiement of Truth and was addressed as Vedanta Incarnate by that great Indian philosopher, now [1967] President of India, Dr. Radhakrishnan.

When Maharishi finished college, Guru Dev accepted him as a disciple at Jyotir Math. "From the beginning all I wanted to do was learn to think like he did," Maharishi has said, "to somehow attune my mind with his." Accordingly, while the ashram's "big huge intellects" (as Maharishi called them) sat all day discussing fine points of knowledge, Maharishi was with Guru Dev helping him answer his abundant correspond-ence. Eventually he gained the master's confidence and was answering all the mail. While familiarizing himself with Guru Dev's thinking he freed his master to attend to his most impor-tant work, teaching. Thus Maharishi assumed the role Trotaka had assumed toward Shankara. The Shankaracharya tradition has always been based on love.

"From my own experience," Maharishi wrote to the teachers,

> I know that there were hundreds of very learned and capable disciples of Guru Dev, yet the task of spiritually regenerating mankind fell to one who was like Trotaka, as distinct from the intellectual giants who surrounded the master....This seems to be the case in the tradition of Jyotir Math—not much learning is needed: just innocent surrender to the master. *This gives us the key to success—we have simple sincere feelings, devotion, a sense of service—and wisdom dawns [Emphasis added]*.

When Maharishi was asked whom he would appoint as leader of the Movement when he was gone, he is reported to have said, "The one who loves most."

When Guru Dev passed in 1953, Maharishi left Jyotir Math and took up residence in Uttar Kashi, on the banks of the Ganges in the foothills of the Himalayas. He said, "After Guru Dev left I felt like a bunch of iron filings that had lost their magnet." He spent most of his time sitting on the banks of the river with a friend. "We seldom spoke," Maharishi said, "there's really not much to say anyway." During that time there was a social gathering at which an Englishwoman had occasion to say to Maharishi's friend, "My good man, you really must visit London."

"Madam," the man replied, "I am London."

Around 1956 Maharishi had a strong premonition telling him to "Go to Rameshvara. Go to Rameshvara." This is a famous temple for the worship of Shiva near Madras, 2,000 miles away to the South. Himalayan Yogis often refer to the rest of India as "a mud," to use Maharishi's quaint expression—a quagmire of confusion, to be avoided if possible. For several days Maharishi discussed his premonition with an old man who occasionally came to visit him. One day the old man said, "Well, you'd better go to Rameshvara if only to get it off your mind."

Everything is within walking distance of you have enough time. On his two-year walk to South India Maharishi taught the meditation technique he had learned from his master. He said, "If Muslims and Hindus can learn Transcendental Meditation side by side, you know I'm not teaching a religion." (The meditation practices and courses Maharishi teaches are grouped together in a non-profit, educational organization. He said, "I could have started a religion, but there are enough religions.) He stayed in a small room near the temple of Rameshvara and went there every morning to pray, still not knowing why he came.

One morning as he was leaving the temple a man approached him, bowed and said, "Do you speak?"

"I didn't know whether he was asking if I had a vow of

silence or if I gave lectures," Maharishi said later, "but anyway I said Yes." On the walk back to Maharishi's room the man explained that he was director of a library in a nearby town and was looking for people to give talks. They sat in the little room, and Maharishi, in a white silk dhoti with his jet-black, shoulder-length hair and full beard, mentioned several subjects he could discuss, and the man wrote them down. When the man thanked him and stood up to leave, Maharishi laughed and said, "Perhaps you'd better leave me a copy of those topics?"

Maharishi's talks drew large crowds that increased each evening. At the end the director told him he had never before met a holy man whose demeanor and behavior so closely corresponded to the dignity of the words he spoke.

(In 1999, thirty or forty students at Maharishi University of Management in Fairfield, Iowa, traveled to India to trace Maharishi's route from Utter Kashi to Madras (now Chennai). This was part of a University course titled "The History of the Movement." When they arrived at the library in Trivandrum where Maharishi spoke more than forty years earlier, they were greeted by the former director's son, now head of the library. Maharishi had instructed him and his father in Transcendental Meditation at the time he gave the lectures.)

When Maharishi reached Madras in 1958, a Council of Spiritual Luminaries was in progress. He was added to the list of speakers from all over India and spoke on the final day. A huge tent had been set up to accommodate the large audiences. Maharishi's talk generated such positive reaction that near the end he said, "If this is the response to my words, I will tomorrow inaugurate a worldwide spiritual regeneration movement." The people leapt to their feet and clapped for more than three minutes. While they were applauding Maharishi turned to the impresario and asked, "Can you maintain the tent for one more day?"

The man said, "Of course, but why didn't you tell me before?"

Maharishi said, "I didn't know until now." Maharishi has said, "I never solicited people to learn Transcendental Meditation. I never had to push myself in. People just came up to me. The entire Movement developed spontaneously." He later told his Transcendental Meditation teachers, "A flower doesn't have to solicit bees. It just radiates its fragrance, and bees show up."

Maharishi went up to Calcutta and collected enough donations for a plane ticket to the United States. When he left he said, "I'll be back with a thousand saints in suits." His first stop was in Burma (non Myanmar) where a group of Buddhist monks had unexpectedly assembled to welcome him. In late in 1958 or early in 1959 he arrived in San Francisco, a city he lovingly called "the first city of the Age of Enlightenment." He had brought only a change of dhoti and a toothbrush rolled in a small prayer rug.

Sometime later he went to Los Angeles. There the Olson family, who had attended one of his lectures and started the meditation practice, invited him to stay at their home. Helena Olson wrote a book about his stay, titled *A Hermit in the House*, later reprinted as *Maharishi at 433*. The Olson's younger daughter vacated her upstairs bedroom for Maharishi. The Olsons repainted it the pale saffron color favored by Yogis.

Maharishi used his time to teach Transcendental Meditation and to begin to put together the Spiritual Regeneration Movement. He stayed up very late because he slept little. (In the profoundly rested state of Self-realization, waking and sleeping often feel much the same.) Late at night he could be seen walking from room to room turning off lights to save electricity. He enjoyed using the telephone. Mrs. Olson wrote that Maharishi used to say, "Thank goodness for time zones, there is always someone awake somewhere." On quiet afternoons he often worked in the glass-walled porch, which overlooked the backyard. The family had several cats. When they gathered in the aura of Maharishi's peace, which they invariably did, he would keep them away by tapping them on their heads with a flower. (He has explained that lower forms of life drain energy from higher forms.)

In 1959, when Maharishi was preparing to leave the West Coast to teach in other parts of the country, an article on Transcendental Meditation appeared in a San Francisco newspaper. It touted the technique as a cure for insomnia. Maharishi said, "That article *set* me on America. I bring the message of eternal life and people are using it to go to sleep."

In the 1960s Maharishi begin to hold large international courses in India to train practitioners of Transcendental Meditation to teach the technique. The Beatles attended one such course, and the issue of *Time* magazine with their photo on the cover was on the coffee table at the Center in Berkeley, California when I went to be instructed. The Beatles had gone to India, not to become teachers but to be with Maharishi and for the longer meditations. But their psychedelic lifestyles may have made the extended meditations difficult. On the *White Album*, John Lennon sang, "I'm so tired / I haven't slept a wink / Think I'll get up / And fix myself a drink." Paul's songs from that time were more cheery. Prudence Farrow, Mia Farrow's sister, was on the course: "Dear Prudence, won't you come out to play / Dear Prudence, greet the brand new day." A former forest ranger from Tuscon named Terry Gustafson—who turned out to be my teacher in Berkeley in 1968—was on that course. He happens to have been the inspiration for the line in *Get Back*, "Joe-Joe left his home in Tucson, Arizona / For some California grass." Donovan was also on that course, a man whom Maharishi still calls "my transcendental musician."

In 1970 I attended a Residence Course for a weekend of extended meditation. The course leader told us Maharishi needed teachers for his rapidly growing Movement. He said any practitioner of the technique can be trained to teach it to others. "All you need is the desire," he said. "If you have the desire, you will cultivate the ability." I was thrilled. After the excitement of San Francisco during the hippie years, I was living quietly with a few fellow meditators on Washington's Olympic Peninsula and looking for something worthwhile to do.

In 1972 Maharishi combined the direct experience of Transcendental Meditation with the intellectual understanding that is the basis of it. This he called the Science of Creative Intelligence, saying that, like any other science, it combined experience and understanding, "laboratory and lecture." I took this 33-lesson video course in the summer of that year. (The Movement had rented space at Humboldt State College in Arcata, California.) I had never seen Maharishi in person. Sometime after the course started, he arrived from Fiuggi Fonte, Italy, where, we were told, he had been taping the Science of Creative Intelligence videos in front of an audience of teacher trainees. These tapes arrived at our course from Italy one by one as Maharishi completed them.

There were about fifteen hundred people at the course. Many of them were already teachers of Transcendental Meditation. We viewed Maharishi's tapes in the gymnasium in the evenings. The night Maharishi arrived was a big one for me. While one of the tapes was playing, there was suddenly a commotion at the door stage right. I didn't know what was happening, but people got up and began to move forward. I couldn't see Maharishi for long minutes, but I could tell he was moving slowly toward the stage. There was a huge crush of people around him, which I finally penetrated. People were giving him flowers. He received them without respect to persons, his smile a continuous glow. He had a double armload of flowers when he climbed the steps to the dais. He put them on a low table in front of the couch, sat down, folded his legs in front of him, blessed everyone with a brilliant smile, and said, "Let's begin on something."

I became a teacher in the Fall of 1972 at La Antilla, Spain, on the Mediterranean Costa del Sol, completing a 10-week course with about two thousand people from all over the world. Maharishi had been monitoring worldwide response to the Transcendental Meditation movement for 13 or 14 years, and at La Antilla he inaugurated the Dawn of an Age of Enlightenment. In response to our comments on the social and political upheavals continuing from the 1960s and the conflict still raging in Vietnam he said, "By definition, the dawn must be inaugurated in darkness." He gave two or three talks a day and certified the new teachers personally at the end of the course. Certainly the most precious experience I've ever had was sitting one-on-one with His Holiness in a small room at the La Antilla facility. He lifted my course application from a plle on the nearby table, looked through it briefly and then looked up at me and said, "So, you have completed all the requirements?"

I said, "Yes."

He gave me a few special words and then with a red marker he wrote "full initiator" on the application.

I taught the Transcendental Meditation technique for many years in my hometown of Fort Worth, Texas, and in Los Angeles in 1975-76 while working at the National Center for the Transcendental Meditation Program. During these years I attended a number of Advanced Training Courses, mostly at Maharishi International University. Maharishi established the University (now Maharishi University of Management) in Fairfield, Iowa in 1971 to provide traditional academic knowledge as a natural extention of the knowledge and experience of the Self. The University is unique in teaching academic subjects as aspects of the transcendental source of all knowledge within, as facets of one over-arcing course of study of the Self . (See the Appendix: *Maharishi Consciousness-based Education*). I also attended Maharishi's courses in Switzerland and Italy.

It was on these advanced courses over the years that I viewed hundreds of hours of Maharishi's videotaped lectures dealing with all aspects of the Transcendental Meditation practice as well as the intellectual knowledge that supports it. These lectures, as well as those I heard in person on courses given by Maharishi, form the basis of this work. Although Maharishi's taped lectures cannot be cited since they are not generally available, I have used quotation marks freely to emphasize the directness with which his statements struck me and the immediacy with which I still remember them, having called them to mind many, many times over the years.

Illumined souls like Maharishi can kindle a fire in a man. I was 31 when I attended that first large course at Humboldt. There has been much bliss and much fretting over failures since then. Evolution of consciousness is both a rocky road and a smooth-flowing river that goes to the sea. For several years after Teacher Training I didn't read anything in any other system of spiritual knowledge. I didn't know it at the time, but I was letting Maharishi's knowledge, and my experiences of transcendental consciousness, establish themselves solidly within me. After that I read everything I could get my hands on. Everything I read, spiritual and non-spiritual, fiction and non-fiction, entered my consciousness in terms of Maharishi's teaching. All great writers are great because they express universal truths—truths that Maharishi teaches in unalloyed form. Truth is in fact everywhere. As one Yogi said, Reality is an "open secret."

I also began to read extensively in the Bible. I was raised in the Baptist Church by religiously liberal parents. I can remember many Sundays after church when my father would say, "Alright son, now here's what they were really talking about." Reading the Bible on the basis of four or five years of Transcendental Meditation, I suddenly seemed to know what they were really talking about. I realized I'd had ears and heard not—and I still do. Again unknowingly, I was following Maharishi's advice that everyone should stay with the religion in which they were raised.

A world teacher like Maharishi cannot teach everyone

everything like a guru in an ashram. He has to speak broadly because his words are going to reach thousands of people. One must learn the subtle points of knowledge on his own and adapt them to his own strengths and weaknesses. Thus, some of the allusions I make to difficulties on the path are things Maharishi would not generally discuss. But I have brought them up to give a clearer picture of what I think true spiritual growth is likely to be like for most us. For example, Maharishi teaches that suffering is not necessary for spiritual growth. I firmly believe in this principle and its importance to world understanding, having experienced it operating in my own life as consciousness continues to develop. But I also feel that, human life being what it is, one who is not conflicted—spiritually or otherwise—has either already "arrived" or not yet confronted his demons.

Maharishi rarely uses others' words. I once heard him quote Plato, and he quoted the British poet William Blake while discussing the necessity of "cleansing the doors of perception." Almost everything he says comes either from his own realization, the Vedas, or his guru. Although Maharishi has an academic background and is a thoroughly modern man, he would probably say that all real knowledge comes from the same source anyway, so why quote. Men like me have to quote others to make their own words clearer.

I have used knowledge from many other sources to explain and corroborate Maharishi's teachings because that's often the way I confirm them to myself. Over forty-five years, the knowledge has flowered on many branches and—as Maharishi has advised—become my own. When one owns a system of spiritual knowledge, he guides his life by the wholes he himself has put together from the parts enunciated by the teacher. Thus, the book is not structured in a sequence of Maharishi's teachings but by my experiences as a seeker in the modern world—by concepts I have entertained and obstacles I have faced, by the hopes, fears and exultations that have caused me to think,

"What did Maharishi say about this?" In this sense the book is mine. Yet the fact remains that if a man lights a torch to guide you through a dark forest, everything you see by that light belongs also, and primarily, to him.

Chapter 1

God, the Devil and the Absolute

Maharishi says that religion is the highest aspiration of man. If so, then it is our deepest need. Highest aspirations must arise from the deepest level of consciousness. To turn our externalized thinking process back toward its source in consciousness is the true meaning of religion—from the Latin *religare*, meaning to bind (*ligare*) back (*re*).

It is the nature of man to believe that a power greater than himself created the world and brought him into it, and that this power is intelligent and purposeful. At bottom, a human being is incapable of believing that the universe is an accident. Even a devout atheist is very religious, Maharishi once said, because he's always thinking about God. As the British poet John Dryden wrote, "No atoms casually together hurled / could e'er produce so beautiful a world."

Where there is disagreement over the existence of God it is usually about a personal God; that is, an *embodiment* of this higher power who knows one and can respond to him as an individual. As we will see, the personal God exists within the manifest field of existence as its subtlest level.

The impersonal, ultimate power, on the other hand, is unmanifest, infinite, and eternally uninvolved with phenomenality. Because it is transcendental (uncreated) it has no beginning or end, and no qualities. To paraphrase Alfred (Lord)

Tennyson, "Gods may come and gods may go, but This goes on forever." The Absolute power is the subject of the "perennial philosophy"—popularized in this era by Aldous Huxley.

Abstract though it is, the Absolute can understood by an examination of relativity. Daylight and darkness are the prototypal relative phenomena. Although the Bible says, "In the beginning…darkness was upon the face of the deep," (Gen 1: 1,2), this condition could not properly be called "darkness" until there was light. The other must be there for comparison. So daylight causes darkness and vice versa. And since they cause each other they have no existence of their own—no real existence. The Real is beyond relativity. It is absolute, changeless, non-material and free of the oscillations that define manifestation.

In its essence, relativity--the world of multiplicity and diversity—is nothing but the transcendental unity which underlies it, the unmanifest unity of the Absolute which is non-material. Thus we find in Hebrews 11:3: "The worlds were framed by the word of God, so that things which are seen were not made out of things which do appear;" i.e., were made out of things which do not appear.

Due to stress in the nervous system our perception is limited only to things which appear; that is, to the surface value of things. But these external forms of relativity are illusory; they are not real because they perish. Anything that ceases to exist at any point obviously has no fundamental existence; whereas, the Absolute, because it is non-physical, has no starting or ending point.

Being non-physical, the Absolute cannot be measured or proved by the instruments of objective (Western) science. But it can be confirmed by subjective science using only the instrument of the mind. This is the essence of the ageless Vedic science as revived in this era by Maharishi. Accordingly, Maharishi refers to the mind as "the best blessing of the Creator" because when properly used, it by itself reveals the Truth. And that Truth turns out to be nothing but Mind. Transcendental Mind, Pure Consciousness, is the only Reality.

Stress and the Devil

There are many interpretations of the Garden of Eden story. In Christian teaching the serpent is evil, and in tempting man he caused the Fall. But a mythological and symbolic reading of Genesis suggests something quite different. The symbol of the fruit-bearing trees suggests that Adam and Eve had everything provided for them. They had nothing to do but enjoy. They were naked and not ashamed and were thus beyond the pervasive duality of relativity. They lived in Paradise.

But it was only a preliminary, or potential, Paradise. Self-awareness was missing.

It is believed that at some point in pre-history man had everything but the ability to think for himself. In *The Origin of Consciousness in the Breakdown of the Bicameral Mind*, the Princeton psychologist Julian Jaynes situates man's transition to self-awareness and conceptual thought between about 1,500 B.C.E. and about 800 B.C.E. This straddles the period in the late second millennium in which Moses is believed to have written the Book of Genesis. Jaynes's thesis of the bicameral mind—in which the brain hemispheres did not communicate with each other, and conceptual and abstract thoughts were heard as voices—is suggested by God's direct, verbal instructions to Adam and Eve. He told them what to think and what to do because they had no consciousness of themselves.

The serpent gave them a chance to make a choice. Metaphysically, the serpent is considered to represent the life force. It is morally neutral; its only function is to promote evolution—in this case the evolution of human consciousness. With the fruit, the serpent taught Adam and Eve the difference between good and evil. Thus it ushered mankind into relativity. And relativity is the only milieu in which man can learn for himself what is good and what is evil, and eventually transcend them again, this time as fully conscious beings. "And the woman said unto the serpent…of the fruit of the tree which is in the midst of the garden, God hath said, Ye shall not eat of it, neither shall ye touch it, lest ye die. And the serpent said unto the woman, Ye shall not surely die: *For God doth know that in the day ye eat thereof, then your eyes shall be opened, and ye shall be as gods, knowing good and evil,*" [Emphasis added] (Gen. 3: 2-5).

If there is a *good God*—a personal embodiment at the subtlest level of material creation—then by polarity there must be an *evil devil* at the same level. In Christianity this is Beelzebub. In Milton's *Paradise Lost*, Beelzebub was the most powerful angel in heaven, virtually equal to God. (He decided, however, that he would "rather rule on earth than serve in heaven.") The duality of this level of the mind is not found in the transcendent. There is no good or bad, only an inseparable mixture of positive and negative that underlies the illusory dualities of Nature.

So where does this leave the devil? In the Impersonal scheme, the role of the "adversary" must be assumed by something else: We are caused to misperceive consciousness as matter (and thus misperceive the world entirely), not by an evil embodiment out to get us, but by stress in the physiology.

Stress has become an increasing concern world-wide in the last three or four decades. But stress is much more than the tension that builds up at work—at least the way Maharishi defines it. He says that stress is "any foreign deposit in the nervous system that limits consciousness." If psychologists are correct in saying that we use only about five to 10 percent of our mental potential—that is, five to 10 percent of our consciousness—then stress becomes a very serious matter indeed. In this light it is little wonder that we have mistaken mind for matter all this time, and Infinity for our finite selves. In the fullest sense of the word, stress "rules on earth." The Biblical "wiles of the devil" are not more insidious than the stress that invades man's body and eventually destroys it. The defining characteristic of both stress and the devil is the ability to hide their own incursions until one no longer knows what is happening to him nor has any means of escape. This is what Christianity means by "lost."

When we were banished from Eden—that is, when we became conscious beings—stress became the bogey that must be overcome if we are to enter the Kingdom of full consciousness.

Because the human mind has both relative and absolute capabilities, the personal and the impersonal God are not ultimately in conflict. The great guru Swami Vivekananda—an Indian representative at the World Congress of Religions in Chicago in 1893—said that a particular genius of Hinduism, and the Vedic culture that predates it, is the ability to believe in a personal God and the impersonal Absolute at the same time and feel no contradiction. This requires use of both hemispheres of the brain. The right side of the brain is intuitive and holistic. It sees the Big Picture; and to the extent we are conscious of this deeper level of the mind, it causes a tendency to favor the impersonal God. The left hemisphere is rational and dualistic and is more comfortable with a personal God who is separate from us.

We must use the total brain if we are to achieve our God-given potential for emotional fulfillment and material prosperity. Every time reason tells us the sun is moving across the sky, we are subtly reminded by the other side of the brain that it's the Earth that's turning; and this does not cause a contradiction. Absolute Pure Consciousness is an eternal unity of intuition and reason (and all of relativity's opposites), which are indistinguishable in that transcendental state, which indeed have no meaning there. This unity becomes a duality when processed by the ordinary human brain.

The Holy of Holies

In the temple at Jerusalem in Jesus' time there was a small, silent room in the center of the building, or in another important place, called the Inner Sanctum. Only the elders (the initiated) were allowed to enter here. Every Christian church today is a reflection of the temple, and also a well-known symbol of the human body: "Destroy this temple, and in three days I will raise it up," John 2:19. And the Inner Sanctum in turn is a symbol for the silent, sacred "place" at the transcendental center of the human mind/body. When we transcend the body of thought in meditation we enter the Holy of Holies, the Church of the Absolute God, without ever going out of doors. This is the "binding back" of religion, which bypasses intellectual concepts, beliefs, and dogma to directly experience the source and goal.

The Christian Trinity of three persons (albeit of the same substance according to the Nicene Creed) clearly situates it in the field of multiplicity, relativity. Maharishi says that, since the personal God (God the Father) is the Creator, this subtlest relative level is where creation begins. This arrangement is similar to the three *gunas* of the Vedas—the three fundamental forces (creation, maintenance and dissolution) that reside at the subtlest level of the phenomenal world. The ultimate, absolute power does not itself create; it is infinite, silent, immoble. It is the perfect stillness necessary that all else may be considered to be in motion.

Maharishi says that the "warming up" of the Absolute is responsible for the three gunas, whose permutations and combinations create, maintain and dissolve the universe. We may think of this "warming up" as the radiation that surrounds a glowing object, like the sun. In the case of the Absolute, this "radiation" is the Creative Intelligence responsible for the universe and is co-equal to the quantum field.

All of us have experienced something analogous to this creative gap between the Absolute and the phenomenal world. In a quiet moment we may fall into a daydream in which we are not aware of ourselves or surroundings. Before the mind can return to activity from this silent, immoble state, there must be a return to consciousness. This is the "warming up" that makes creative thought possible.

The common notion that prayer involves the individual and something external to him is true only if our awareness is limited to the surface self. But at the deepest, transcendental level of consciousnss—the all-enveloping Self—the personal God is known to exist within us. Thus, in reality, when one asks for aid in prayer, he is not petitioning something external. Rather, he is identifying individual needs to be fulfilled from the infinite reservoir of his own Self.

Chapter 2

The Ocean of Consciousness

"One unbounded ocean of consciousness in motion." This is how Maharishi describes the nature and structure of the universe. Only consciousness exists. The incessant motion of its various frequencies results in the myriad, apparently physical, forms. As the physicist John A. Wheeler said, "There is nothing in the world except empty curved space. Matter [is the] curvature of space."

Maharishi refers to the ocean of consciousness and the fluctuations of its frequencies as *Veda-lila*, the play of Veda. In one of its aspects, Veda is transcendental knowledge, pure intelligence; in another, it manifests in vibrational frequencies of energy and information. In this state, which Maharishi calls Creative Intelligence, it functions at the level where Being (Pure Consciousness) becomes manifest. This is the interface between the unchanging Absolute field of existence and the relative world of forms and phenomena—the warming up of the Absolute.

The Bible says, "In the beginning...the earth was without form, and void." Since creation followed, there must have been something that was awake, conscious, in that formlessness. In Eastern spirituality this transcendental wakefulness is called Pure Consciousness or Atma. It is pure both because of its infinite (thus unalloyed) nature and its status as eternal perfection.

On its basis, Maharishi teaches, and on its basis alone without the agency of manifest action, the universe comes into being as a *conceptual* rather than a material reality.

Since pure wakefulness is infinitely aware, it is of course aware of itself. In this awareness an observer, an observed and a process of observation come into being. That is, because Pure Consciousness knows itself there is a knower (called *Rishi*); because it knows itself there is also a process of knowing (*Devata*); and likewise there is an object of knowledge (*Chhandas*). This interaction within the Transcendent is called Self-referral, the factor that metaphysics says is necessary for creation. But as we continue to discuss creation, *we must bear in mind that the creation exists only in the Transcendent and remains forever transcendental as nothing but the Creator.*

The world certainly appears solid. But of course an appearance depends upon the perceiver as well as the perceived. And in this case, the physicality of the universe has nothing to do with physicality and everything to do with our perception.

But if the creation is unmanifest, then what is this that we see, touch and interact with every day? The answer is that this is That. This is the transcendental creation we are looking at, but we can't see it *as such* until the mind returns to its natural state of transcendental consciousness.

Rishi's immoveable wakefulness is the silence—and its transcendental "act" of Self-referral is the simultaneous dynamism—from which the universe is created as the transcendental unity of these two extremes. The universe is an on-going process of elaboration—an eternal process of transforming silence into dynamism. Every organism, object, thought and action is nothing but the silent ocean of consciousness in conceptual motion. But as our perceptual acquity has been worn down over the long lapse of time and by the stress of human life we have come to perceive the subtle as gross and the unmanifest as manifest. We see only the dynamism (Wheeler's "curved space") while missing the silence—which is Pure Being, the bliss of which the world is made.

Maharishi has said, "Bliss and bubbles of bliss are the only two elements to life." This striking statement stands as a promise of the most intimate and joyous experience of silence and dynamism possible, an experience that awaits us all. When the great guru Paramahansa Yogananda was asked about the bliss inherent to life, he called it "ever-new joy."

The eternal expansion of the transcendental universe is caused by Rishi's Self-referral looping back to his primal silence. "Curving back upon my own Nature, I create again and again," Krishna says in Ch. 9 v 8 of the *Bhagavad-Gita.* "Creation and administration of creation are both a natural phenomenon on the basis of My Self-referral consciousness."

Thus is established an infinity-value which is uncreated (silent) and a point-value which is "created;" that is, dynamic. The unity of these two extremes of existence is understood by the fact that the alternation of two opposite vaules without lapse of time amounts to simultaneity.

Our present life is pre-structured from our thoughts and actions of the past, and can be re-structured at any moment, Maharishi says. This re-structuring, or re-creation, occurs in the circular phenomenon of looping back to our infinity— Krishna's curving back to his own nature. It is as though we are piloting an aircraft at an increasing distance from the airport while remaining in contact with the control tower for directions. Maharishi explains how this restructuring happens by using two Vedic words, *Agni* and Atma.

He says that Vedic Sanskrit (the language in which all of the Vedic literature was written down) is a transcendental language. It is made up of what, at one level, are virtual sounds, sounds that occur in the uncreated. Sanskrit is a language in which name (sound) and form (creation, or dynamism) are two aspects of the same thing. Creation begins when the open-mouth sound "Ah" (the first sound of Rig Veda, which we could call the sound of infinity) collapses to the point-value, or stop-value, "K", which is the second sound of the initial word Agni. (Because of a Sanskrit rule of euphony, the "K" changes to "G".) When the Vedic seer Madhuchchhandas heard the first frequencies of creation at the transcendental level of his own consciousness, they were the sounds "Ah" and "K" and, along with "Ni", were simultaneously the universal creative impulse and the *deva*, or demigod, Agni. In the "Ni" sound is structured the on-going aspect of creation, the looping back of the creative process.

The creative collapse from "Ah" to "K" is explained in Rig Veda 1.164.39,

Richo akshare *parame vyoman*
yasmin Deva adhi vishve nisheduh.

Focusing on the first two words, Maharishi translates this as follows:

"The verses [**Richo**] of the Veda exist in the collapse of fullness [that is, in] the **kshara** of "A" in the transcendental field, the Self, in which reside all the Devas—the impulses of Creative Intelligence, the Laws of Nature responsible for the whole manifest universe."

Maharishi calls this the "master verse" of the Vedas. Perhaps because it declares that all of the 40 or more voluminous treatises of Veda reside in its first syllable, as does the whole universe!

The name/form principle of Sanskrit does not mean that the ordinary spoken word ceates the object. But at the level of the Transcendent the word and the object occur at the same time. ("And God said let there be light, and there was light.")

As divinely formed (conscious) beings, we have the ability to curve back to our own nature and create again and again. We do this habitually through the spotaneous process of seeing and knowing—we call to mind our faults with intent to eliminate them. But this uniquely human activity is nonetheless a pale reflection of the divine connection Nature has set up for us. The word Atma, with its infinity-to-point movement ("Ah" to "T") and its curving back ("M" to "Ah"), describes the creative Self-referral we experience in meditation when we transcend thought to Pure Consciousness, which is Atma.

Because of the name/form factor, even ordinary pronunciation of the word Atma gives a faint experience of Pure Consciousness. The sound of any Sanskrit word—such as *shanti* (peace)—gives a faint experience of that. Atma is defined as Pure Consciousness, but the real meaning is what occurs when we transcend thought, or to a lesser degree when the word is spoken. The popular chanter/singer Krishna Das says that the meaning of the Sanskrit words he sings is the experience you have when you hear them.

With the creative curving back to Self that is Transcendental Meditation we are in large measure freed from analyzing our faults and trying to eliminate them. Through regular practice they thin out and disappear like clouds when the sun comes out.

In Ch. 9 v. 8 of the *Gita*, Krishna also said, "Creation and administration of creation are both a natural phenomenon on the basis of My Self-referral consciousness." With experience of Pure Consciousness, Nature heals (administrates) the human organism it creates. The evolution of consciousness rectifies the personality holistically and in a powerful way that begins immediately. Through the ability God gave us to see and know, everyone eventually curves back, or binds back, to the experience of direct self-healing.

What Hath Rishi Wrought?

Rishi, Devata and Chhandas (observer, process of observation, observed) are not separate things. In fact they are nothing at all but the unbroken wholeness of Pure Consciousness, which remains eternally separate from, and uninvolved with, phenomenality. However, when Pure Consciousness sees itself, vibrational frequencies, sound, are set up ("consciousness in motion"). These frequencies are technically matter because matter and motion imply each other. The division of unbroken wholeness into Rishi-Devata-Chhandas is a concept, as we have said, the concept that produces the illusion of material creation. It is a product of intellect, a human ability that can never by itself divine the ultimate, but by which we experience all of life in terms of a knower, known and a process of knowing.

The vibrational frequencies of Veda, in almost infinite permutations and combinations, are the only real constituent of the universe. They result from the awareness of consciousness of itself. We may also say they result from perception by deity, which is the first creative act. This principle is a tenet in the philosophy of George (Bishop) Berkeley, the eighteenth-century century Irish philosopher, and summed up in his famous aphorism *"esse est percipi"*: to be is to be perceived. This is also the primary source of the principle in quantum physics that observation of the quantum wave function (frequencies of consciousness) brings sub-atomic particles into being (perceptual creation). From these frequencies of consciousness are structured all the rocks and trees, rivers and mountains, all elements, and everything in the animal, vegetable and mineral kingdoms. We transform these vibrational structures of the world into our own personal illusional solid objects by a deficiency of perception. Deepak Chopra, M.D. says in *Perfect Health*:

> Western physicists already acknowledge that at the deepest level of the natural world we find the quantum field, which defies our commonsense notions. There is no solid matter in it, for example.... The hard edges of any object, such as a chair or table, are an illusion forced upon us by the limits of our vision. If we had eyes tuned to the quantum world, we would

see these edges blur and finally melt, giving way to unlimited quantum fields.

The eminent British neurologist and Nobel laureate Sir John Eccles said, "there is no color in the natural world and no sound—nothing of this kind; no textures, no patterns, no beauty, no scent. Sounds, colors, patterns, etc., appear to have an independent reality, yet are, in fact, constructed by the mind. All our experience of the natural world is our minds' interpretation of the input it receives." Dr. Eccles could well have offered a rainbow as an example of this. A rainbow does not exist in the sky; it exists in consciousness: Wavelengths of light are bent into different frequencies by moisture in the air, but what appear to be external color, form, meaning, etc., exist only in the perceiving mind. And the conditions of our consciousness determine what we perceive. Likewise we might think that an orchestra produces music on the stage. Actually it produces a variety of specialized vibrations that become music only when they reach the human mind.

The mystery of mysteries has always been how the One becomes the many by being misperceived. But when the surface mind gives way to transcendental mind, the mystery dissolves into awe of a power so great that the three worlds arise on the basis of its mere existence.

But Pure Consciousness's contemplation of itself is more elaborate than the simple observation we have discussed. Because Pure Consciousness is omnipresent, its self-observation may be thought of as being ramified infinitely, so that every *wave* of its Self-referral awareness becomes a *particle* of creation. This is the primal instance of the famous particle/wave paradox of modern physics. Matter is particulate or wavelike depending on observation; the particle becomes manifest (dynamic) through observation of the wave. In this way, the frequencies of Pure Consciousness have become the furniture of the world.

The particles of creation are unmanifest—uncreated, except

by our own particular vision of the manifold radiations of Being; they are our minds' interpretation of the input it receives, to use Eccles's words. In his commentary to Chapter 2, v. 28 of the *Bhagavad-Gita* Maharishi says:

> The phenomenal presents the manifest state of life, while Being is of unmanifested transcendental nature. According to the findings of modern physics, all matter has only phenomenal existence and is in reality formless energy. Both in its previous state and its present obvious form, matter is nothing but pure energy.

That what we take for matter is essentially unmanifest consciousness—waves of energy and information—was graphically illustrated by Itzhak Bentov, in his "look through a supermicroscope" in Stalking the Wild Pendulum.

> Now let us magnify a piece of bone. Very soon an orderliness will emerge: highly ordered bone crystals embedded like jewels in webs of long molecular strings. Everything is vibrating….Some more magnification will give us an even better look at this crystal: We see the atoms weaving back and forth like a field of ripe wheat blown by the wind. They move in unison and in beautiful rhythm. Acoustical energy is flowing through the crystal.
>
> Next we focus on the atoms. At first, they appear as little shadowy balls vibrating about fixed points in the molecule. As we magnify, we see less and less. The electron shell [orbit] has somehow dissolved, and we are looking at a vacuum. As we further magnify, we see something tiny moving about. We focus on what we suspect is the nucleus of the atom, located in this vast space within the atom.
>
> If we take the diameter of the nucleus of a hydrogen atom to be 1 mm., then the diameter of the electron orbit will be about 10 meters, a ratio of 1 to 10,000, and the intervening space is vacuum.
>
> As we zero in and further magnify the vibrating nucleus, it seems to be dissolving. We are looking at some shadowy

pulsation; some more magnification, and the nucleus is almost gone. We are sensing the pulsation of some energy; it seems to be a rapidly pulsating field. But where did the bone go? We thought that we were looking at a solid piece of matter!

Bentov's imaginative use of a microscope shows that we see matter the way we do because our limited awareness in effect removes us so far from it. The Tibetan Lobsang Rampa (who was not working with a microscope, even an imaginary one like Bentov's) said, in *You, Forever,* that if we were far enough away from the universe it would appear solid and if we could see the skin of our hand closely enough it would look like the universe on a starry night.

Because consciousness is everywhere, when we become fully conscious we can be conscious anywhere. When we can be inside the observed object as we are inside the universe, we will see it according to its true nature.

The vast and scattered spheres, tiny in comparison to the space between them, exist because they are observed. If no one saw them, on what basis could they be said to exist? "To be is to be perceived." Universal creation is a cooperative venture involving an observer.

Veda and Veda-lila

The principle of Rishi-Devata-Chhandas is not a philosophy. It is a cognition that occurs at the level of Creative Intelligence (the vibrations of Veda), which is the quantum field. From this subtlest level of the thinking process, when the rishi's consciousness further settles into the uncreated wholeness of the Absolute, it is self-evident that That, alone, is.

Anyone can experience this level of existence. Maharishi says anyone who can think a thought can experience the subtlest level of creation (and beyond) because that level is merely his consciousness in its simplest, most natural form. He says that active thought, by definition, contains quieter thought within it, as the ability to run contains within it the ability to walk, and the ability to walk contains the ability to stand still.

Thus, because of the structure of consciousness from gross to subtle, the process of transcending thought is effortless. In Ch. 2, v. 40 of the *Bhagavad-Gita* Krishna says, "In this Yoga no effort is lost and no obstacle exists." (The Sanskrit word "Yoga" means union.) For thousands of years those who have undertaken to teach Enlightenment have almost universally believed that the nature of the mind is to wander from object to object, like a restless monkey, and therefore must be brought under control. In his commentary on this verse Maharishi says that the mind wanders not by nature but "for the possibility of happiness that the object provides. *Thus it does not actually wander from object to object but moves from a point of lesser happiness to a point of greater happiness,"* [emphasis added]. This being the case, what is needed is not control of the mind (as we have mentioned) but a meditation technique that takes advantage of the mind's natural tendency to seek happiness.

Maharishi blames man's continued suffering on misconceived attempts to control the mind in the name of God. Focusing on the symptom (wandering) rather than the cause (the search for fulfillment), teachers have advised control techniques which only frustrate the mind and make it more restless. This increased restlessness, of course, has seemed to confirm the original misconception generation after generation.

In the same verse Krishna also says that "no effort is lost" in this technique for God-realization. Maharishi says this is because

> no effort is needed!…Since the field of eternal freedom is absolute bliss, the process of uniting the mind with it, once having begun, comes to completion without loss of energy or effort. It does not stop until the experience is full…What is necessary is only to begin to experience the increasing charm

on the way to transcendental absolute bliss. As in the case of diving, one has only to take a correct angle and let go—the whole process is accomplished in an automatic manner.

Taking the "correct angle"—following the simple instructions that give the mind the first step inward—is Maharishi Transcendental Meditation.

The distinction between the wandering behavior of the mind and its true, bliss-seeking nature is a subtle one. But a small error at the beginning of a proposition can become a huge mistake over time. In this era man labors under the tragic misconception that fulfillment of his aspirations (if that is even possible) necessarily involves a struggle against his own unruly mind (as if the real purpose of the mind that conceives one's hopes and dreams is to deny their fulfillment). This notion not only permeates society but is institutionalized at the highest levels of philosophy. Suffering, hardship, and failure are regarded as inherent to life. "'To err is human' is a common proverb," Maharishi once said ruefully, "as though man was born to make mistakes;" when by the design of his consciousness and nervous system, the true promise of man's birth is perfect freedom in union with God. The belief that our own mind somehow stands in opposition to this punctures the balloons of hope that sustain us both here and hereafter, and has led countless generations down the road to dusty death.

The glory of Lord Krishna's pronouncement that there is no obstacle to union with God is that it casts down the great myth that man must struggle to make something of himself. Society praises to the heavens these hard-won victories in the lives of its most vigorous members, whereas man's true greatness and the symbol of his God-born dignity must be (although it is counter-intuitive in today's world) that fulfillment of his desires comes easily, without effort. In his essence, man is not a human being who occasionally has divine experiences, but a divine being in exile who usually has human ones.

The ultimate cause of mistaking the nature of the mind is obvious: Those who misperceive the reality are not in union with God. Only those who are established in the bliss of Absolute Being can know that that bliss is what the mind seeks. It will never occur to one whose mind is still wandering in relativity. The success that Transcendental Meditation has enjoyed worldwide over these 50 years, establishing Maharishi's name as a household word, is validation of his epochal insight. This capacity for unobstructed union with God is the true meaning of Rousseau's "born free".

In *Perfect Health* Dr. Chopra recounts an experience of a practitioner of Transcendental Meditation:

> I feel the boundaries of the mind being pushed out, like the ever-widening circumference of a circle, until the circle disappears and only infinity remains. It is a feeling of great freedom, but also one of naturalness, *far more real and natural than being confined to a small space* [emphasis added]. Sometimes the sense of infinity is so strong that I lose the sensation of body or matter in an infinite, unbounded awareness, an eternal, never-changing continuum of consciousness.

(The expanding circle mentioned above is an after-the-fact metaphor. Transcendental Meditation involves only thinking a certain thought in an effortless way that allows it to become increasing refined and dissapear into the Transcendent.)

The term Veda refers not only to the vibrational frequencies at the subtlest level of the mind (mentioned above) but to a vast collection of literature comprising some forty systems that contains the unsprouted seeds of knowledge lying dormant at that same transcendental level. Among these systems are *Sankhya* (intellectual knowledge of Self-realization), Yoga (experiential knowledge of Self-realization), *Ayur-Veda* (science of health), *Jyotish* (Vedic astrology, or the mathematical science of prediction), *Sthapatya-Veda* (architecture to elicit the positive natural influences in creation), *Gandharva-Veda* (music to enhance the vibrational frequencies that obtain at different times of the day and at different seasons of the year), and the *Yoga Sutras of Patanjali* (union with God, including cultivation of supernormal abilities such as Yogic Flying®). Maharishi is currently reviving all of these systems. Other Vedic systems include the *Puranas* (stories of the exploits of Enlightened beings), *Itihas* (world history, which includes the Indian epics the *Mahabharata* and the *Ramayana*), and *Sama-Veda* (sounds to produce evenness of the intellect).

The Vedas are the oldest extant records of human wisdom on earth and derive not from human thought but, as above, from cognitions of the functioning of Natural Law at the Vedic level, where the mind achieves invariant status. They are infused knowledge, knowledge direct from God that Christianity distinguishes from acquired knowledge. Revealed or discovered at the dawn of man's introspective capabilities, the Vedas have been credited with man's survival as a species over time; for in essence they are his own higher consciousness. As this knowledge has spread around the globe from pre-history, it has been re-shaped into many different philosophies, religions and knowledge systems to suit time, place and culture. For example, the Sanskrit word *dyan*, meaning meditation, (from Patanjali's *Yoga Sutras*) became *chan* when it reached China in the sixth century and *zen* when it arrived in Japan. With each cultural transfer something of Veda is lost and knowledge deteriorates, necessitating periodic revivals like Maharishi's.

It is not difficult to understand, or at least visualize, that the world is nothing but consciousness in forms. If God alone existed "in the beginning" there was nothing from which to make the world except his own non-material Self. Thus we find in the *Upanishads*: "I am That [Pure Consciousness]; thou art That; and all this is nothing but That." A great contribution of quantum physics to world knowledge is that it confirms through objective science what subjective science has seemingly always known. The Austrian physicist Erwin Schrödinger, called the father of quantum theory for his formulation of the quantum equation in 1926, wrote in *My View of Life*:

> Consciousness is the singular for which there is no known plural.
>
> Consciousness and the external world are one, and the same thing.

(Schrödinger's work brings modern objective science and ancient Vedic Science together. In an article on how modern thought has been influenced by Vedic traditions, Subhash Kak wrote, "Before he created quantum mechanics [Schrödiger] expressed his intention to give form to central ideas of Vedanta, which therefore has had a role in the birth of quantum mechanics." Schrödinger thought like John Wheeler ("What we observe as material bodies and forces are nothing but shapes and variations in the structure of space.") and like Shankara ("All happenings are played out in one universal consciousness.")

Maharishi refers to the primal pure wakefulness—the unity of Rishi, Devata and Chhandas—as *sanghitā*, ("togetherness" in Sanskrit). This is the transcendental Pure Consciousness at the source of thought within us, where the Oneness that comprises the Self and the object is experienced. This unity of subjective and objective, inner and outer, on the level of direct experience is the acknowledged goal of all of philosophy.

"The world is as you are," Maharishi says, "own Pure Consciousness and the world will be yours." If the singularity of sanghitā is fully established in one's day-to-day awareness, he cognizes the primal unity of the three divisions within and throughout the object—the "physical object" that his conditioning and personal style of perception have taught him to see. But if the observer is still vibrational, the observed is known only as a solid object and appears to be essentially different form other forms of matter.

"When the mind is disturbed, the multiplicity of things is produced, but when the mind is quieted, the multiplicity of things disappears." Notice that this statement (from the *Ashvaghoshas*, an eighth-century Zen work) clearly does not say that the multitude of things *seems* to arise when the mind is disturbed, but that they do arise. It clearly implies that the mind and the world function as essentially the same thing. There is a Zen story of two monks walking along a road carrying the banner of their monastery. One monk is saying that the banner is waving. The other says, no, the wind is waving the banner. Just then a wandering monk happens by and says, "It's neither; it's your minds that are waving."

At a certain point—called sanghitā samadhi (everyone together Enlightened)—the dynamic universe is said to withdraw, like a tortoise withdraws its limbs, and leave only cosmic wakefulness. A new universe would be based on the karma (vibrational residue) left over from the previous one. So, one may ask, what produced the karma for the first universe? In the *Science of Being and Art of Living* Maharishi writes,

> Karma acts as a force of wind to produce a wave of the mind in the ocean of unmanifest being....If there were no influence of karma, the mind would not be, but without the mind...the karma or action cannot be produced. The mind is born of karma and creates karma, and karma is born of mind and creates mind....The seed produces the tree and the tree produces the seed. Metaphysics' solution is that the cycle of mind and karma has no beginning and no end.

A scenario in which creation is periodically withdrawn and then restarted may not be completely satisfying, however, because it leans too heavily on the materiality of creation, which by now is becoming suspect. But there is another view of what is going on. Maharishi said karma creates a wave of mind in the unmanifest. This disturbance, or localization, in the field of undifferentiated mind is what we call creation; for it causes us to localize and separate objects and events. ("When the mind is disturbed the multiplicity of things is produced.") Then creation is an illusion that overlays the Reality of undifferentiated (transcendental) mind. This illusion is called *maya* or *yogamaya*. Hindus believe it is the power of God (Krishna) to hide Reality. ("Maya" comes from Sanskrit roots meaning "that which is not.") This view holds that, in fact, because the Creator is non-physical, there can never be a physical creation, that creation is impossible because something cannot come from nothing. This turns out to be a central teaching of one of the earliest and most respected Vedic systems, Sankhya (mentioned above as the intellectual knowledge underpinning Self-realization). Krishna uses Sankhya for his "text" in Chapter Two of the *Bhagavad-Gita*. From this point of view, maya hides not a creation but the fact that there is not one. It hides the Uncreated by the disturbance of our minds.

The dissolution of the universe at the point of sanghitā samadhi—when all are conscious enough to appreciate Reality—clearly implies that the physical universe goes on the basis of ignorance, illusion. In his commentary to verses 15 and 16 of Chapter Two of the *Gita* Maharishi says, "This ignorance, and the bondage born of it, keep [physical] life in motion. The wisdom of Sankhya cuts asunder the bonds of ignorance and allows life to be lived in its natural state of eternal freedom." With respect to the Real/unreal question, "eternal freedom" means that one enjoys a state of perfect silence while observing the illusory world swirling around him—Shakespeare's "tale told by an idiot, full of sound and fury."

"Sankhya," wrote a Hindu historian, "is the most significant philosophy that India has produced." In the doctrine of the author, Kapila, "for the first time in the history of the world, the complete independence and freedom of the human mind were exhibited." (Will Durant, *Our Oriental Heritage.*) Kapila said that if God is perfect, he has no need to create a world, and if he is not perfect he is not God; that the "created" is nothing but the Creator; and that God could not possibly have created so imperfect a world, so rich in suffering, so certain in death. (It seems that Kapila would leave these things to be created by our illusions.)

Either the world is real—and full of sadness, pain, and heartbreak—or it's an apparation arising from the mayic confusion of our own minds. In the one case we are blameless, helpless victims; in the other, we are at fault but have a way out.

But why didn't God just make everything bliss for us from the beginning? Some would say he did and that he sends people to tell us about it. Or perhaps it must be this way because we wouldn't experience the bliss without the contrasting pain. We couldn't enjoy the brilliant summer day without the darkness that preceded it.

(For many years Maharishi used the terms unmanifest and manifest to distinguish between the two fundamental phases of existence—uncreated and created. These two pairs of terms are virtually interchangeable with silence and dynamism. And now, possibly because of the rapidly growing proficiency in Yogic Flying—in which the impulse to lift up (dynamism) occurs *within* the silence of Pure Consciousness—he uses these terms almost exclusively. He seems to be emphasizing the unity of silence and dynamism rather that the distinction between unmanifest and manifest.)

Kapila said the creation is nothing but the Creator. As we have discussed, we look at uncreated silence but see only the dynamism that, in the final analysis, is a concept.

All of this magnificent activity of the universe occurs in the unmanifest state like a dream in which a lot of action may occur without any of it ever being expressed, or externalized. Like this, the creation can be understood as the dream of Brahm. And like any other dream, its reality (what it may be and what it may mean) can be known only by entering into the consciousness of the dreamer. When that happens, all This is known to be nothing but That.

Kapila saw ordinary reality as entirely derived from perception, saying that our sense organs and thought give to the world all the reality, form, and significance it can ever have, and that what the world might be independently from them is an idle question that has no meaning and can never have an answer.

So instead of a periodic creation and dissolution of a physical universe, we seem to have a periodic rise and fall—keyed to the collective consciousness of humankind—of the illusion that one exists. Leftover karma as the cause becomes the disturbance of our minds, Krishna's yogamaya. This is Veda-lila, the game of hide-and-seek God sets for us. Krishna the unmanifest, wrapped in his maya, is within and without everything we see, throwing alluring sidelong glances our way.

The End of Philosophy

Ever since man began to think—that is, since there was man—there has been a distinction between knower and known, between oneself and the things around him. At some point farther down the road, perhaps based on intimations of our immortality, we intuited a God. In relation to this God (Rishi) we became the known (Chhandas). Nature became the link between man and God—his creation and our milieu. The laws of Nature that we discovered functioning in our mind and all around us, which are "the way things work," became the process of knowing (Devata) by which a conscious unity could be effected between above and below.

Thus God and man and law became an extension of Rishi, Chhandas and Devata, and philosophy was born as a quest for their re-unification as the goal and meaning of life. Our yearning for our home in sanghitā is the most compelling evidence that a fundamental unity is in fact realizable; for a yearning cannot arise on an abstract basis but only from something already known but forgotten.

Throughout the current phase of history, the West has been ascendant. But prior to the fall of Rome, the West as we know it was hardly at all. Many of the important things the Western world has struggled to learn were already known if we had been able to look eastward into the right, intuitive, hemisphere of our brain. One thing Western philosophy has proved is that the left brain is for computers, and the right brain is for philosophy. (We'll discuss the characteristics of the brain hemispheres in the next chapter.) Although the left, rational hemisphere can *understand* the ocean of consciousness, it cannot by itself experience it. Duality structures our consciousness, and a divided vision cannot see a unified world. The intellect is only a part of the mind and thus, by definition, blind to wholeness.

However, Western philosophy has come up with a way to measure the effectiveness of its theories. It is based on the principle of simplicity, on the understanding that the theory with the fewest parts is likely to be the most complete (like the seamless garment of Christ). Although William of Occam never said, "The simplest theory that covers all the facts is the most accurate," he did say, "It is vain to do with more what can be done with fewer," which became the maxim, "Entities are not to be multiplied without necessity," which has become the modern version of Occam's Razor. Consciousness, since it is the only thing both existent and non-material, is a convincing candidate for the simplest thing there is. (If you look up "simplicity" in the dictionary you'll find a picture of consciousness.) Consciousness also accounts for everything: Being non-physical, it is infinite and eternal; it is intelligent (mind) while possessing a unique ability to be mistaken for matter. Nature makes it easy for us; it doesn't multiply entities unnecessarily.

The only requirement is that we take it as easy as Nature makes it, and that means seeing with the simplest form of awareness. This is its most settled and expanded state and reaches far beyond the puny efforts of reason and logic. As William Blake wrote, "You [are led] to believe a lie / When you see with, not through, the eye." The universe is known for what it really is only at the level where peace passes understanding. Perhaps the greatest distinction that the faculty of reason holds in the scheme of things is that what it can't see is probably the Truth.

Accepting the ocean of consciousness as Reality requires putting reason on the shelf and adopting the mind-set of the early Christian Father, Tertullian, who is famous for saying, "Credo quia absurdum. Certum est quia impossible est." I believe because it's absurd. It's certain because it's impossible.

Chapter 3

The Time Factor

From the lofty precipice of sanghitā, the Cosmic Fool missteps and descends into manifestation, trailing clouds of glory. But he is also carrying a lot of karmic baggage, and thus dualized at birth he is primed for conditioning by society.

It is said that an infant senses no physical separation between itself and its mother. At the very earliest age, this would include objects in the wider environment as well. This is a kind of unity, a lingering sanghitā; but actually it is merely a state of non-difference, because the infant as yet has no awareness of self to unify with anything.

When self-awareness develops, which is awakening into this life, it brings with it a sense of separation from the environment. And from this beginning—one more incarnation of our immortal soul—we journey through the slough of duality until we come full circle to an experience of unity with the surroundings. Our long-time conceptual separation is then resolved into a profound experiential realization of the Self as sanghitā; that is, as present in all objects of experience as their only constituent and as the only constituent of all existence. This is the final Self-referral. The physical universe is known as nothing but Myself.

I was once favored to hear Maharishi say, "The moon is a part of me." The awesome meaning of this statement and its ineffable glory is inconceivable to most of us now. But it is clear enough to make us agree with him when he says, is his matter-of-fact way, "this is a goal worth seeking."

Our journey picks up speed with a second awakening in which we see a division within ourself, a separation between two parts of our being. We learn from adults, particularly from parents and teachers, that we have a bad self. In some long-forgotten moment, someone shouted, "Stop doing that!" and we split down the middle. The soul has forgotten these first really horrible things that told us something was wrong with the world; in the bright light of new hope, darkness was unable to gain a foothold in memory. Yet because this experience was driven deep before we had critical judgment it is perhaps the most important experience in anyone's life. It is the practical basis of our receptivity to social conditioning, as we will discuss shortly. It is also the source of our belief in our inadequacy and, by extension, our mortality.

In his famous novel *Steppenwolf*, Herman Hesse presents a character whose awareness of his two selves is so stark that he thinks of himself as half man, half beast—a wolf of the Steppes. The book was set in Germany in the years between the World Wars and was popular in America in the 1960s, as it dealt with the spiritual/material division in the self and society, and the conflicts between a middle class and a disenfranchised creative fringe. Also, much of it took place in a "magic theatre," which was easily mistaken for psychedelia.

The Legacy of Industrialism

The problems of Steppenwolf (Harry Haller) are those of his era and culture. (Goethe said, "A man's vices are those of his times; his virtues are his own.") "Human life is reduced to real suffering," Harry Haller says, "when two ages, two cultures and religions overlap....There are times when a whole generation is caught in this way between two ages, two modes of life, with the consequence that it loses all power to understand itself."

There couldn't be a clearer picture of America and the industrial West in the 1960s: The transition between the industrial age and the information age, the clash between the mainstream and a counter culture, and the advent of Eastern religions. (Maharishi stepped off the plane in San Francisco into the epicenter of these changes.) It was the beginning of the end of mass values and the onset of the more diverse electronic era. The oft-told fragmentation of family, school, workplace and religion still affects people in deep, powerful ways. In particular we have been forced to establish a new moral code with very little tradition (particularly in America) to work with. How well we have done this is to be seen in the alcoholism, drug abuse and general directionless of society today—the loss of the power to understand ourselves.

Sensory indulgence has long been regarded by Yogis as the behavior most injurious to life in general and to spiritual development in particular. The industrial society that arose around 1700 bequeathed us a sensory-indulgence problem in a peculiarly modern form. When the rise of the factory and the monetary system split the individual into producer and consumer (where before we consumed what we produced) it destroyed our sense of wholeness and self-integration and forced us, perhaps for the first time in modern history, to search for artificial means to assuage our sense of alienation.

But the effect of this on society is much deeper than the addiction problems of a relative few. These are only the distillations of a widespread predisposition to look to externals for fulfillment. The habit of looking to the world for fulfillment is more deadly in the long run than any other addiction or social problem it may lead to. This habit is our legacy from the industrial era.

Of course there is a tendency to romanticize our pre-industrial past, and compared to the 1700s and 1800s it was certainly an extended period of disease, poverty, homelessness and bitter struggle against the elements. If one believes that life inevitably gets better, the agricultural era was an even sadder scene than the huddled masses of industrialism. However it is questionable that the latter was an improvement in the standard of living in the larger sense. At least we got through agriculturalism with a sense of our individual wholeness. And that cannot be claimed for any epoch since. That is to say, as Charles A. Reich did of industrialism in *The Greening of America*,

> The bonds of affection and concern between men were broken by the harsh imperatives of competition. As pecuniary relationships replaced ties of tradition, custom, religion, and respect, men obeyed authority only when forced by economic necessity or penal laws, and in consequence modern crime became the obverse face of society. Man was uprooted from his supporting physical and social environment and, like a polar bear in a city zoo, he would from then on suffer an alienated existence.

In the agricultural era, we satisfied the needs of the body by what we grew ourselves. We lived with nature, integrated with earth and sky. The senses served as a balance point between mind and body, and when the needs of the body were satisfied, the attention naturally turned to the higher needs of the organism. This provided a sense of wholeness and self-sufficiency that made artificial indulgence of the senses generally unnecessary and undesirable. Only after we compartmentalized ourselves in factories and offices and city blocks did the senses turn in upon themselves and become a major cause of our problems.

> Activity of all kinds [Reich says] was rooted in folk and religious culture which developed 'irrationally' [non-rationally] and without conscious design in response to human needs. That world, both in Europe and frontier America, was destroyed in the making of our modern world.

Although this destruction was, ultimately speaking, an evolutionary necessity (as we shall see), the thought of that vanquished world can be saddening for anyone who has ever struggled to let go of "conscious design" and live the spontaneous life. For one knows that life is richer in that holistic state and that this doesn't mean abandoning consciousness, only this present consciousness and its pitiful designs.

In *The Third Wave*, Alvin Toffler says that of all the factors that came together to produce industrial civilization—new technologies, literacy, population growth, etc.—the most important was the split between producer and consumer. "The shock waves of that fission are still apparent today," he says. When we no longer consumed what we produced but turned it into money to purchase products from others, something entered our life that tempted us away from attention to our higher needs— namely the money. The most important and far-reaching effect of this was to provide us with something we could save and store over time as a substitute for personal growth, something tangible by which we could measure our individuation in the world.

That we can save and store means that there is never a natural end to work—the seasons of the year have been paved over. There is always something we can be doing. The anxiety caused by a stifling environment and artificial ways of living prods us to "forage" constantly. The break in the natural immediacy of producing and consuming—which is the medium of exchange—disrupts the energy that flows in an organic cycle from production to consumption to production. As a result we never really satisfy the body and lift our attention higher. Reich says,

> The most profound import of the commodity system and technology was on man's own individual being....Man was not merely alienated from environment and society, he was alienated from his own functions and needs. [His] most basic

activity was dominated by the most impersonal of masters—money. [He] became alienated from himself as money, not inner needs, called the tune...[and] began to defer or abandon his real needs.

As a result we have significantly lost the ability to distinguish between real nourishment of body, mind and spirit and the temporary excitements of fast food, disturbing entertainment and elicit desires. We think we are nourishing and comforting ourselves when in large measure we are merely surfeiting the senses to kill the pain of our discomfort. The senses, which are intended to bring exaltations of joy to the emotions, are instead being used to salve emotions strained and frayed by wanton use. In this state, which is now nothing less than a social addiction, the body can never be satisfied nor the real needs of the organism met.

When looking to externals for fulfillment became an established habit of society, another wedge was driven between the active, thinking man and his silent, all-knowing Self. This "object referral" approach to life has virtually extinguished the light of Pure Consciousness within. The object orientation that came on so strongly with the factory, the machine, and the money about three hundred years ago has not only alienated us from our physical and social environment and our personal needs. It has effectively robbed the Western world of the ability even to conceive of a Self-referral process and a transcendental consciousness.

But Nature itself is working to rescue us from our confusion. The pendulum has swung as far as it can go. The present chaos has a purpose—and that is creation of order on a higher level. Chaos turns out to be a function of Nature's overarcing order. It is the universal principle of dissolution necessary for life to be recreated on a higher level.

The individual is subject to this as well as the society. The individual experiences chaos as a temporary loss of direction and meaning in life. The concepts by which he guided his life break down and Nature intervenes with a reassertion of order. Consciousness expands into a kind of cloud of unknowing from which—as discontent gives way to new intentions—another generation of workable concepts is brought forth and progress continues in a more evolutionary direction.

The present collective confusion mirrors that of large numbers of individuals. It is through its members that society periodically exchanges one set of guiding concepts for another, going through chaotic periods in which the old must be let go before the new can be grasped. It is also through society that Nature steps in with great prophets like Krishna, Buddha or Christ when catastrophe threatens.

In the agricultural era our emotional and spiritual needs were not as evolved as they are now. We have higher to reach than we did then and are further burdened by our appetites. Our frustrations in this effort have been so manifest as to give the name "Age of Anxiety" to the twentieth century. Yet because of our higher evolution, the spiritual order to come from the present chaos will be much higher than our agricultural selves could have reached. For, the senses notwithstanding, the advance in evolution we have made is a result of the three hundred years of industrialism and its left-brain rationality.

The People and the Times

As painful as the process has been, we have learned as a civilization to function on a higher level of the left brain and have thus taken another step toward the ultimate synthesis of the rational and the intuitive. Although these different modes of thought are found in both sides of the brain, the left and right hemsipheres are generally characterized respectively as, rationality and intuition, parts and whole, analysis and synthesis, reason and passion, sense and sensability, etc. These complementary opposite forms of mental activity alternate like the two feet as mankind strides along the path of evolution. As a new millennium gets underway, it is this higher foundation of rationality that is giving us the ability to function on a higher level of intuition than previously; for the second foot cannot come forward until the first is firmly planted.

The period around 500 B.C.E. was one of balance in the West. The German historian Karl Jaspers called it the "axial age," or pivotal age. Significantly, this was the era of Buddha and Shankara in India, Confucius and Lao Tze in China, Zarathustra in Persia, and Pythagoras and Heraclitus in Greece. It is as though this balance-point brought forth the light of *dharma* (righteousness, mental virtue) to guide us through the next 2,500 years. From the pivotal point we entered upon a thousand years of Greek rationalism guided by left-brain thought. But around 500 C.E.—through the dialectical principle of thesis/antithesis—the dominant mode of thought shifted to the right brain of intuition, and the West entered the religious Middle Ages. After about another thousand years the energy had moved back to rationalism and spawned the Renaissance. This latter mode of mental functioning picked up speed with the Industrial Revolution about 1700.

It seems that the turn of the present century heralds a resurgence of intuitive, holistic thinking and that Nature's millennium-long steps of progress have been cut in half by the increasing pace of life since the Renaissance.

In 1980 Toffler wrote: "In all intellectual fields, from the hard sciences to sociology, psychology and economics...we are likely to see a return to large-scale thinking, to general theory, to the putting of pieces back together again." At the onset of the industrial age, Rene Descartes stimulated scientific advancement with the publication of *Discourse on Method*, which was "to divide each of the difficulties under consideration into as many parts as possible." But now, as Toffler says, "It is beginning to dawn on us that our obsessive emphasis on quantified detail without context, on progressively finer and finer measurement of smaller and smaller problems, leaves us knowing more and more about less and less."

As a civilization we don't reach higher until we are engulfed in problems. But when we do, we discover, like the individual, that order is a spontaneous result of chaos. At the moment the moon loses its light it starts to become full. Problems seem larger to a conscious and capable society than to a dull one. To see problems clearly is to see the solutions.

It was the science of the industrial era that led to the discovery that time itself is a creation of man. Einstein proved that time is not a given in Nature. Time is only the interval between events, and in the Uncreated there are no events. There are no events at the Absolute level of the mind, the silent source of thought. Time is a product of perception of relativity.

Through the force of evolution, Nature is constantly infusing Pure Consciousness into the human mind, a flow of transcendental energy in which the opposite mental capabilities of reason and intuition, analysis and synthesis, etc. are unified as one. However, in our dual consciousness in the field of time, this energy appears as two opposite modes of mentality that alternate in apparent time and produce the historical periods we have just discussed.

There is a broader time frame, however, that shows Nature at work to bring about infusion of Pure Consciousness.

The *yugas*, or world ages, were identified by Vedic seers millennia ago. *Kali* yuga, lasting 432,000 years, is the age of darkness. *Dwapara* yuga brings more light into consciousness. *Treta* yuga brings still more light. And *Sat* yuga is the Golden Age, the widespread realization of Truth, sanghitā samadhi. According to this cycle of ages the earth is currently Kali yuga.

This scheme is much too vast to be meaningful to the ordinary mind. And according to Sri Yukteswar Giri, guru of Paramahansa Yogananda, it is in error. In the introduction to his book *The Holy Science* written in 1894 Sri Yukteswar presents a simpler yugic cycle of 24,000 years, which corresponds to the precession (backward movement) of the equinoxes through the zodiac, year by year. He says that in the motion of the our sun and solar system around the galaxy they revolve around another star system which causes them to periodically approach and separate from a galactic center called *Vishnunabhi,* "which is the seat of the creative power, Brahmā, the universal magnetism." He says that Brahmā also regulates dharma, "the mental virtue of the internal world."

In about 24,000 years, the earth passes under the influence of the four yugas in succession—Kali yuga lasting 1200 years and the other three 1200 years longer than the previous one—2400, 3600 and 4800. This totals 12,000 ascending years from Kali, Dwapara and Treta to Satya. In the following 12,000 years the yugas descend from Satya until the nadir of Kali yuga is again reached. Sri Yukteswar's yugas have the same general characteristics as in the larger scheme. In Dwapara yuga, awakening from the darkness of Kali, man is able "to understand the finer matters and electricities." In Yukteswar's scheme the last previous nadir of Kali yuga (the earth's farthest point from Vishnunabhi) was in the year 500 C.E. By this system we are able to observe the changing abilities of human consciousness in our time.

Maharishi has said that the nadir of human consciousness will be when man believes that progress in religion requires suffering. The period around 500, after the fall of Rome, was the onset of the Dark Ages in the West and a time when some of the more zealous Christians, desiring to emulate Christ's suffering, practiced extreme self-mortifications—throwing themselves naked onto thorn bushes, practicing self-flagellation and having themselves buried upright in the ground to their necks.

Twelve hundred years after the nadir of Kali yoga, as the

Earth approached closer to the galactic center, came the dawn of ascending Dwapara yuga in 1700. Sri Yukteswar explains that a hundred years prior to this, man had begun to glimpse the finer matters and electricities characteristic of the Dwapara age:

> About 1600 A.D., William Gilbert discovered magnetic forces and observed the presence of electricity in all material substances. In 1609 Kepler discovered important laws of astronomy, and Galileo produced a telescope. About 1670 Newton discovered the law of gravitation. In 1700 Thomas Savery made use of a steam engine in raising water. Twenty years later Stephen Gray discovered the action of electricity on the human body.

By the dawn of Dwapara yuga in 1700, the Renaissance-period had brought us to the Industrial Revolution.

Within the span of each yuga (1200 years, 2400 years, etc.) there is a dawn and a twilight. The dawn and twilight of Kali yuga are a hundred years each and those of the following yugas are a hundred years longer than in the previous one. Thus, after its dawn in 1700, Dwapara yuga proper began in 1900.

Einstein's Special theory of relativity, published in 1905, was a profound exposition of the "finer matters and electricities" providing knowledge that helped create the atomic bomb. In the 1920s quantum theory was formulated, revealing truths about the nature of matter and the mechanics of creation that man is still struggling to understand. The quantum technologies of the twentieth century (television, fax, computers, wireless telephones, etc.) are qualitatively different from the technologies of industrialism for their source in the knowledge of electronics (as distinct from electricity).

(ParamahansaYogananda apparently does not regard the Universal yugic cycle mentioned above—of 432,000 years, etc.—as being in error, as did his guru. In *Autobiography of a Yogi* he says only that Sri Yukteswar "discovered the mathematical application of a 24,000-year cycle to our present age," and refers to it as the Equinoctical cycle. Elsewhere, Yogananda explains, "Western astronomers have postulated an equinoctial cycle of our solar system as consisting of 25,920 years, determined by the present rate of motion. According to Hindus, however, that rate varies at different stages of the cycle.")

Some advanced spiritualists, particularly in India, believe that the Equinoctical cycle was known before Sri Yukteswar. Be that as it may, it is possible that Maharishi was making reference to it when he spoke of Guru Dev's sojourn in the forest as the cultivation of a light that would last ten thousand years: By the current Equinoctial cycle the pinnacle of the coming Sat yuga is 10,500 years distant. Indeed, when asked how long the influence of Transcendental Meditation would last in the world, Maharishi said, "for ten thousand years." In this light, Guru Dev's birth in 1868, a few years before the beginning of Dwapara yuga proper in 1900, takes on special significance. And this age can be said to have begun in a spiritual and religious sense when Swami Vivekananda appeared before the World Congress of Religions in 1893.

(Yogananda says, "the ascent and decline of the ages is not a circular evolution that ends as low as it began; it is spiral." This would allow reconciliation of the Equinoctical cycle (with its obvious applicability to the present times) with the hoary tradition of the larger cycle: The smaller cycles, being spirals, would bring higher levels of collective consciousness with each revolution until the Sat yuga of the Universal cycle is eventually reached.)

Since the epochal opening of man's mind to the more powerful, electrical level of existence in 1900, however, life on earth seems to have gotten worse almost immediately, beginning with the world wars. It is true that we have used our new knowledge of quantum theory (the most successful theory in the history of science) for positive things, but the destruction that has been wrought seems to weigh heavier. In addition, our growing mental power over the last hundred years has been used for more kinds of crimes and mischief than we could formerly even have imagined. These things can perhaps be explained by a natural delay in the influence passing from Vishnuhabhi.

As the sun approaches the galactic center of Vishnunabhi, consciousness is expanding. Quantum understandings are percolating upward into collective consciousness to evolve thought and behavior. Many thousands of people worldwide are experiencing Being on a daily basis through Maharishi Transcendental Meditation, acting as agents of Nature's evolutionary infusion of Being into the collective mind. These things prompted Maharishi's concept of an Age of Enlightenment in 1972. But the approach of the sun and solar system toward the "warming" influence of Vishnunabhi, is subject to an anomaly that is also found in the Earth's movement around the sun.

Each year on December 21 the Northern hemisphere begins to move toward the light. But because of the lingering karma of Winter, two or three months pass before the Spring warm-up begins to take hold. Like this, our current Dwapara earth is still "cold" from the karma of the Kali age. The collective body has not yet stabilized the new consciousness for completely responsible use. Our newfound awareness and power are being projected through minds and nervous systems still used to old ways of doing. We are reaping the whirlwind of chaos between the old and the new. Maharishi says that the earth is currently undergoing a "phase transition."

(Noting the growing success of Yogic Flying practice—which we will discuss in Chapter 10—Maharishi said that Kali Yuga is giving way to Sat Yuga. But the yugas invisioned by the ancient seers cannot be altered by any event occurring within them. Rather, Maharishi's pronouncement seems to suggest that the real, the non-temporal, Sat Yuga exists in human consciousness. The Prime Minister of Maharishi's Global Country of

World Peace said recently that "Maharishi has brought Sat yuga in the midst of Kali yuga." Sat yuga arrives with individual Enlightenment. To the pure, all things are pure.)

Having tasted the hor d'oeuvres of the coming banquet, our civilization, like a starving man, wants dessert now. In ignorance of the long process through which the world is passing, we don't see that our new energies and knowledge are only a beginning. We are like the sophomore who, because he has learned to think, thinks he knows everything. The crimes against ourselves, others and the environment we are now witnessing seem to confirm Maharishi's assertion that "all crime is an attempted shortcut to fulfillment."

The most conscious members of society are often the first to be influenced by the new mental power and are often the worst troublemakers. We see the officers of investment companies bilk their clients out of billions of dollars, finding no good reason why they can't "have it all now." Drug users are often highly evolved souls who get waylaid shortcutting to the ecstacy that altered consciousness promises. Priests, who have devoted their lives to God-realization through celibacy, can no longer restrain themselves. Senseless drive-by shootings and mass murders reveal the lethal frustration resulting from unfulfilled expectations, as do terrorism and suicide bombing. Businessmen and developers, for the first time in history, have the technology to totally remake the face of the earth, but are as yet unable to comprehend, or to care, that their prosperity results in the earth's impoverishment. Likewise, politicians worldwide have not only the power to send thousands of boys to their deaths in war for their own political ambitions, but the power to destroy the social and environmental fabric for the benefit of the fewer and fewer who vote. Modern spiritualists have their own problems in violating their personal rules and resolutions, which can also be seen as the tendency to take shortcuts.

The current global problem can be understood as one of

ego. But if we think in terms of extinguishing the individual ego—as spiritualists and psychologists often do—we fail to understand its full meaning. The sense of "I" can never be taken from an individual even by death. The solution to individual and social problems lies not is shrinking the ego but in learning how to let it expand to the cosmic ego, which sees the larger picture.

In looking for the real relationship between the times and the tendencies of those who inhabit them, we run up against the chicken-and-egg question: Are we being governed by the times or are we ourselves the determining factor? Certainly each of us was born into precisely this world because we needed the experiences it has to offer. But the characteristics of an era can be none other than those of its people. These headlong times, then, represent the needs of large numbers of people who are on the cusp of great change from chaos to order.

"It was the best of times, it was the worst of times," wrote Dickens. If these times are a trial, they are also an opportunity for the soul. The challenge is in consciousness and the way we apprehend the realities of life at the beginning of the new millennium. It all centers on the question of the rapidity of change; for to live in times like these requires rapid evolution of consciousness. Every era is one of more rapid change than the previous, since the pace of life always increases. But the increase appears uneven, so that the ever-rising line of change is steeper in some periods than in others.

Historians use the terms "modernity" and "modernism" to describe the current era. These words signify an awareness within civilization of a significant break with the past, a clear-cut qualitative change caused by an increased pace of life. The agricultural era lasted thousands of years but the industrial era only three hundred. In 1980 Toffler expected the current electronic age to last "a few decades." In our era change seems to be moving upward like a straight line. As a result we have been forced to radically reorganize the framework of our consciousness from the simpler mode of even a generation ago. The "mass mind" of the 1950s has yielded to social opinions that are starkly less uniform and more contradictory. "Instead of receiving long, related 'strings' of ideas, organized or synthesized for us," Toffler says, "we are increasingly exposed to short, modular blips of information—ads, commands, theories, shreds of news, truncated bits and blobs that refuse to fit neatly into our pre-existing mental files." We must reclassify and reintegrate information constantly. Modernity means to

> keep an eye out for those new concepts or metaphors that sum up or organize blips into larger wholes....Instead of merely receiving our mental model of reality, we are now compelled to invent it and continually reinvent it. This places an enormous burden on us. But it also leads to greater individuality.... Some of us crack under the new pressure or withdraw into apathy or anger. Others emerge as newly formed, continually growing, competent individuals able to operate, as it were, on a higher level.

In this era, being able to operate on a higher level of awareness often means regarding truth as relative rather than absolute. Modernity seems to mean that truth is not something written in stone but rather a stepping-stone to the next level of knowledge. Ultimate Truth is absolute, but day-to-day truth, especially where spiritual knowledge is concerned, is what feels right at the moment, what can be integrated with who we are now. Even though we may be misled from time to time, an attitude of acceptance will ultimately yield certainty. Maharishi says that habitual doubting can only lead to a lot of doubtful knowledge.

The present confusion is a spur to spirituality, but that is only part of the story. The other part is that our level of evolution makes Enlightenment possible in this lifetime. The stick and carrot of this generation are the threat of annihilation and a vision of the Holy Grail. For many, life is not unlike Harry Haller's, who is "outside all security and simple acquiescence... whose fate it is to live the whole riddle of human destiny heightened to the pitch of a personal torture."

We might say that time will tell whether Nature has stepped in with another great prophet. But it is certain that it has produced a generation of people who need great knowledge. (Maharishi has said that revival of the Supreme Knowledge is incumbent upon this generation because we are the ones who let it lapse centuries ago.) What is happening is not an objective phenomenon. The people and the times are two views of the same process. We are the cause of what we will overcome. The problems we face are our own. They will be solved as each one of us comes out of his own chaos by dreaming a new direction and a new certainty. In this way, through its individuals, civilization is poised for deep crisis, rapid change and great advancement.

Conditioning and Logical Dualism

The sudden censure by our elders and the shock that opened the chasm of duality within us is the first lesson in our conditioning by society. To put it another way, conditioning can't begin until unity is broken. Carlos Castaneda said that every adult is a teacher who explains the world to us up to the point that we *get it.* The Scottish psychoanalyst R. D. Laing is not quite as generous. He said that a child has to be rendered insane before he will accept the horrors of this world. Nor is society able to give us anything but the dualism that is its "only stock and store," like Poe's raven who could only utter the death knell, "Nevermore." The more advanced a society is, the more effective is it's conditioning. Primitive cultures have been notoriously sloppy about destroying the self. The more technology a society possesses, the better it can advertise its message—which is essentially the separation of man from himself, Nature, and God.

As the universe is structured in unity, society by its very nature is structured in duality; duality is the All in All, the essential and only constituent. As relates to society, duality is "the Word" in the Gospel of John: *"In the beginning was Duality, and Duality was with society and Duality was society....All things were made by It; and without It was not any thing made that was made."* Because the virus of duality enters below the horizon of our consciousness, there is virtually no limit to its expansion and its power. Duality is the cause of fear in the individual and in the civilization at large. In Ch. 1 v. 28 of the *Gita* Maharishi quotes the *Upanishads*: "'Certainly fear is born of duality.' Whenever and wherever there is a sense of two, fear or suffering can exist."

Logic (rationality) is half of our God-given potential of consciousness and as necessary for successful living as intuition. At its highest level, human logic is the transcendental logic of Nature. Logic leads to problems and dangerous half-solutions only when it overbalances or excludes non-logical knowledge. This can hardly be avoided when people undertake to govern others. The natural diversity that arises from individual needs tends to be ignored or excluded as inconvenient. Instead, people are placed in the either/or categories that define logical dualism. Of these categories, which are essentially objective, one ultimately comes to be labeled "good" and the other "bad" on the basis of which is more useful, not to the individuals concerned, but to society. Of the categories "employed/unemployed," for example, the employed person is not only a greater benefit to society, he is a better person. One whose life is dependent on technology contributes more to the Gross National Product than one devoted to personal improvement, and is therefore a better person. Likewise, food consumption based on convenience produces a better person than does that based on nutritional judgment. (This "political correctness" is found to some extent in all societies, even those based on folk tradition.)

As a result of this, great numbers of people are guilty one way or another in the eyes of society. Diversity itself, regardless of its content, becomes suspect. (When this pass is reached, signs spring up here and there reminding us that we must "celebrate diversity.") The most capable people often must alienate themselves from society psychologically or physically in order to pursue goals which are not only natural to them but are basic to the organism in an absolute sense, such as health, professional calling or development of consciousness. As the Russian writer Aleksandr Solzhenitsyn said, "If you spend as much time each day on self-development as on combing your hair, you are thought strange." In addition, many sensitive people are sacrificed to the god of dualism that, unknown, has taken over their minds.

Logical dualism is a result of the left hemisphere of the brain dominating the right—the parts overriding the whole, analysis taking over from synthesis. If you look at a photograph of a human face upside down, you can see all the parts—you know whether the eyes are narrowed or open, whether the corners of the mouth are turned up or down, if there is a smile or a frown, etc.—but you are blind to the whole that is greater than the sum of these parts. In effect you can't see the *face*.

The choice of logical dualism is always for what appeals to reason rather than intuition, what jibes with the parts but not necessarily the whole. What doesn't fall into the category of reason falls out of the social mind and its worldview: The non-logical becomes illogical, and the non-rational irrational. The intrinsic values of things are often overlooked—trees are either good for building houses or good for nothing. The deeper meanings of behavioral choices are obscured—a child either goes to school or ends up a failure. One is either doing something practical or wasting time. Reality comes to depend on objective proof alone: The logical dualist must go outside and look in the window to see if he's at home. "Ignorance," said the

Zen writer D. T. Suzuki, "is another name for logical dualism."

We are conditioned to accept a world of only two intellectual dimensions. In *The Aquarian Conspiracy*, Marilyn Ferguson recounts an episode from the Victorian novel *Flatlanders*. The characters are assorted geometric shapes living in an exclusively two-dimensional world. As the story opens, the narrator, a middle-aged Square, has a disturbing dream in which he visits a one-dimensional realm, Lineland, whose inhabitants can move only from point to point. With mounting frustration he attempts to explain himself—that he is from a domain where you can move not only from point to point but from side to side. The angry Linelanders are about to attack him when he wakes up.

Later that day he attempts to help his grandson, a little Hexagon, with his studies. The grandson suggests the possibility of a third dimension—a realm with up and down as well as point to point and side to side. The Square proclaims this notion foolish and unimaginable.

That night the Square has an extraordinary, life-changing encounter: A visit from an inhabitant of Spaceland, the realm of three dimensions. At first the Square is merely puzzled by his visitor, a peculiar circle who seems to get larger and then smaller. The visitor explains that he is a Sphere. He only seemed to change size because he was moving forward and backward in space. Then realizing that argument alone will not convince the Square of the third dimension, the exasperated Sphere creates for him further experiences of depth. The Square is badly shaken. He experiences dizzy, sickening sensations so acute that he cries out, "Either this is madness or it is Hell!"

"It is neither," the Sphere replied. "It's knowledge."

Logical dualism is the most potent weapon of the maya of Eastern spirituality and the devil (the deceiver) of Christianity. Taken over by the antichrist of dualism, even the Church teaches the ultimate distinction between man and God, and therefore the separation of man from Nature and from himself. And the ordinary man sees nothing but what society has to offer, never realizing that we become what we behold. In its dark wisdom, society garners virtually invincible power by creating a division at its most basic level: in the minds of its constituent members. For as Beelzebub well knows, a "house divided against itself shall not stand [alone]" (see Matt. 12:24-5).

Society functions as an organism of itself, with its individual members acting as its cells, like bees in a hive. Like any organism, its primary objective is survival. Thus all its energies are directed toward getting its members to perform in the social interest, and above all to keep them from breaking away for their own purposes. The violent objections a person may exhibit toward the eccentricities of another are sometimes from a perceived threat to society, which he unconsciously considers his larger body.

The organism's intelligence is about that of its average member, which makes it dangerous enough, but in the long run dangerous even to itself. For it is prey to the same critical oversight of the ordinary man: It fails to see that in the end survival and Self-realization are the same thing. (Neither the individual nor the group survives without realizing the eternal.) Instead, in its survival-anxiety, society erects a barrier to the one vision that could save it—resolution of its inner duality; with this, however, it would have to share its power with the individual. Therefore all societies eventually die. But not (we believe) the wider civilization. The essential difference between organism society and a hive of bees is that people have self-consciousness as well as collective consciousness, and thus the capability to transcend the organism. Civilization endures because individuals separate themselves from society in the matter of their own survival. As Thomas Merton said, "You can't have order without saints."

But since our consciousness is in part collective, we are

complicitous in the fact of society and what it is. Moreover, if we become what we behold in society, we also behold in society what we are. For we created it. Its dualism can be none other than our own. Ignorant of our birthright as unbounded beings, we trade it for the world's meaningless fragments and only later awaken to our loss. We make the bargain of Faust, which Goethe recognized as that of Everyman.

And the bargain gets better each generation. Faster and more far-reaching technology offers more efficient ways to cover Nature's eternal bliss with the ocillations of pleasure and pain, and offers less temptation to try to discover who we really are. But the good news is, as in Faust, there is a second chance. Paradise is not forever lost. Social conditioning, owing to both the people and the times, is subject to the reaction of Nature.

Chapter 4

Good Self / Bad Self

The duality within us that made us susceptible to social conditioning is now quite clearly formed into what we generally think of as a good self and a bad self. Both were created in the fateful instant that our "error" was brought to our awareness.

The "bad" self was created by awareness of it. Prior to this it had only potential existence in our karma. Maharish says, "Karma of the past life is responsible for the mind's identity in the present life.... [but] karma is inert [potential]." The potential nature of this karma makes it analogous to the electron unmanifest in the quantum vacuum state brought into materiality and set in motion by the physicist's awareness.

If we could have known beyond a doubt at age three that nothing on the so-called negative side of life has any ultimate reality, but is only the outcome of thought and action based on illusory perception, we would have never seen it or become it. We would have remained pure like the three monkeys of Indian fable: Hear-no-Evil, See-no-Evil, and Speak-no-Evil. In legend, Gautama the Buddha, being a prince, was sheltered from the world and remained a pure soul. He had no need to seek spiritual development until the day, feared by his father, that he saw an old man, a sick man and a dead man. Only when this negativity entered his consciousness did he feel the need to quest the spirit.

What we believe determines what we are in a more complete way than most of us can imagine. In *Science and Health* Mary Baker Eddy tells of the case of an Englishwoman reported in the prestigious British medical journal *The Lancet*. Tragically jilted by a lover in her early years, she became insane and believed herself still living in that moment, waiting for his return. Thus living without consciousness of time she grew no older and manifested no signs of age. At 74 she had a youthful face with no wrinkles and no grey hair. A group of American visitors who saw her at that age guessed that she was under 20! Mrs. Eddy said, "Years had not made her old because she had taken no cognizance of passing time....She could not age while believing herself young. One instance like [this] proves it is possible to be young at 74...decrepitude is not according to law, nor is it a necessity of nature, but an illusion."

Of course we can lose our illusions without losing our mind. Indeed, letting go of illusions reveals the supermind.

From the point of view of cause and effect, the negative tendencies deposited in my past karma are the cause of my present imperfections—awareness of them has nothing to do with it. But this logic does not take into account the paradoxical field of potential existence—it allows only the existent and the nonexistent. At the deepest level of the mind, however, awareness is the cause of manifestation (as in the case of the electron). Thus my awareness determines my life, and therefore (paradoxically) determines the character of my past karma. In fact present awareness and past karma are the same thing. "Mind is born of karma and creates karma," as Maharishi said (Ch. 2, "Veda and Veda-lila").

In *Unconditional Life*, Dr. Chopra tells the story of a physician friend of his who died of cancer two months after seeing a spot on his lung in an x-ray. Chopra's attention was drawn to the mind/body connection when he later happened upon a chest x-ray of the man taken five years previously that showed the same spot, only slightly smaller and a little more vaguely defined, that was not diagnosed. Although the man was a heavy smoker, the cancer grew hardly at all in five years; yet when he came to believe in it, in killed him in two months. He could live with the disease but not the diagnosis. Satchel Paige was a scientist when he said, "Don't look back, something might be gaining on you."

Awareness of duality binds us to relativity. At the same time, it gives us the ability to free ourselves from it. If we are not lost we can't be found. Our individual lives follow those of Adam and Eve to a significant extent. Early in life we ate of the Tree of the Knowledge of Good and Evil, lost the paradise of unconsciousness and gained the opportunity to become fully human.

In a very real sense, the Garden of Eden mythology is a story of the left hemisphere of the brain (reason) at the critical period when the world was losing its dreamlikeness in the late second millennium B.C.E. Adam and Eve were banished to till the soil and earn their living by the sweat of their brow. This can be understood as a metaphor for cultivating our new ground (our new foundation) in relative consciousness, ultimately developing the perfect balance of reason with the right-brain of intuition in an ascending spiral toward final unity with God, which will this time be conscious (as we discussed in Ch. 1, "Stress and the Devil"). Like Adam and Eve we have to be taken apart before we can be put together on a higher level of reality. By awakening we learn that something is lacking. This makes us aware of our cosmic situation and makes action possible. Yet because of the force of evolution this "action" is spontaneous.

In Chapter Three we saw that our first sense of difference from our surroundings is destined to close in unity with our higher Self accompanied by the realization of the Self as the ultimate constituent of all things. Actually, because this unity has never been broken, but is only an illusion caused by stress and misperception, our evolution requires only the settling of consciousness to its simplest form in the eternal silence of Being. And since consciousness settles and expands naturally through evolution, this is inevitable. The dawn of self-consciousness is the question to which the full sunshine of Self-realization is the inevitable answer. Self-awareness is the God-given first act of seeking, of which Jesus said, "Everyone that asketh receiveth; and he that seeketh findeth" (Luke 11:10). Swami Vivekananda's dictum—"Arise, awake, and stop not until the goal is reached"—is not, in essence, a rule to be followed but an eventuality that cannot be avoided.

Likewise the Ten Commandments, as commands of God, are laws impossible to break. The Commandment "Thou shalt not kill" cannot be violated: The Self is eternal and does not participate in the come and go of life. In Chapter Two of the *Bhagavad-Gita*, Krishna says to Arjuna, who is reluctant to attack his beloved kinsmen in battle even though they have usurped his throne:

> These bodies are known to have an end; the dweller in the body is eternal, imperishable, infinite. Therefore, O Bharata [Arjuna], fight! He who understands him to be the slayer, and he who takes him to be the slain, both fail to perceive the truth. He neither slays nor is slain. He is never born, nor does he ever die; nor once having been, does he cease to be. Unborn, eternal, everlasting, ancient, he is not slain when the body is slain.

Neither is it possible to commit adultery or any of the other sins because the Self is ever uninvolved with the relative field of existence. We suffer from sin because we believe it is real, as Arjuna suffered debilitating indecision by believing in the reality of death. If we saw and knew and lived the utter unreality of sin, there would be no possibility of committing it. To put this another way, sin is impossible to the knower of Reality. All violations of Natural Law result from the illusion of our separateness from the perfection of sanghitā, and they will not cease until the illusion is seen for what it is and we are freed from it. Handed down by the great I AM, the Ten Commandments are a vision of life in Enlightenment—and the monumental proclamations of a soul on fire with the realization that it is not possible for the soul to sin.

The Third Awakening

As discussed in Chapter Three, we first awaken to a separation from mother and environment and then to a separation within ourselves. In accordance with natural laws governing consciousness, the more awareness one has the deeper will appear the division within the self and the intensity of the discomfort this causes. As Aristotle said in the *Ethics*: "In proportion the thing is perfect the more it feels the good, and so the pain."

The third, or higher, awakening is the awakening by Grace, based on native consciousness. The Grace of God, in one form or another, is the only thing powerful enough overcome the pervasive conditioning of duality and restore our lost God-consciousness. The third awakening is also based on our past good karma. Karma and Grace function identically in a critical way: Both denote an unknown factor that determines our life, a source of seemingly undeserved mercy as well as brutal justice. Maharishi says, "we may think of life as determined either by God or by our past karma." ("But," he hastens to add, "we have the ability to re-determine it at every moment.") From the standpoint of this lifetime, karma and Grace are the same thing. But either way, at some point we receive the blessing of experiencing the split within us as intolerable.

This is the beginning of the spiritual path. We have stepped beyond the shallows of the surface mind—which the psychologist Joseph Chilton Pearce characterizes as self-reflective only; meaning that it cannot see beyond its own limitations and so gives the illusion of wholeness. From the break-up of the seed the plant sprouts. We are no longer the ordinary man whose life, though difficult, is acceptable. Either by faith or its complement, necessity, we have embarked on the pursuit of an ideal that we can't be sure exists until it is found and can't be proven to anyone when it is.

"Faith cometh by hearing," St. Paul said, "and hearing by the word of God" (Rom. 10:17). In the Universe of Self we have been discussing, this is an inner voice, and the message is that we are already complete except for realizing it. "Let me know [realize] myself, Lord, and I will know thee," is a well-known prayer of St. Augustine. The usual interpretation of this is that one knows God only by contrast (polarity) with his own human misery, and therefore only from afar. But the complete version of the statement makes Augustine's meaning clear: "Seek for yourself, O man; search for your true self. He who seeks shall find—but, marvel and joy, he will not find himself, he will find God. Or, if he find himself, he will find himself in God."

Harold C. Gardiner, in his introduction to Augustine's *Confessions*, calls this Augustine's "great discovery." The final identity between God and man is expressed here, and was of course taught by Christ ("The Kingdom of God is within you," Luke 17:21). In the tenth chapter of John, Jesus says, "I and my Father are one." When the Hebrews took up stones to stone him for blasphemy—"thou, being a man, maketh thyself God."—he could have responded in several ways. He could have recanted. Or he could have said, "I'm God, but you're not." Instead, he chose to equate the Real nature of his accusers with his own Real nature realized as Christ: "Is it not written in your law [Psalm 82: 6], 'I have said, Ye are gods'?" This was a guiding principle of early Christianity until it was decided that a Church wouldn't be necessary if the Truth were known.

In terms of the third awakening, the internal division in Hesse's Harry Haller was more a product of evolved consciousness than objective fact. His agonies resulted from a sickness of the times that "by no means attacks the weak and worthless only but, rather, precisely, those who are strongest in spirit and richest in insights."

The more consciousness one has, the more aware he is of his faults. But since expanded conciousness equates with improvement in the self, the faults themselves will be less. Natural Law creates order in the individual and society, and counteracts entropy, by one's being more aware of his failings as he evolves, because this continually stimulates the evolutionary impulse. This is in service of the Natural Law that the more consciousness expands, the more it will expand. Jesus said, "For whosoever hath, to him shall be given, and he shall have more abundance." The reverse is also true: "But whosoever hath not, from him shall be taken away even that the hath," (Matt. 13:12). At the low end of the consciousness spectrum, one is less and less aware of his faults as they multiply. Thus his consciousness and capabilities continue to decline. If Natural Law functioned in the reverse, as we sometimes think it ought, one would be less aware of deficiencies as he made progress. But if so, the impulse to evolve would decline along with growth, and progress would be reach a limit. By the same token, a poorly evolved person would clearly see his faults and be moved to rise above them until he reached the level of the other. This would be equal distribution of energy, an aspect of entropy; and this is what Natural Law cannot abide. Promotion of evolution is its purpose. There must be people to make discoveries and keep society moving (even if it means that "Ye have the poor always with you," Matt. 26:11). And above all, the human organism must reach is limitless potential of awareness so that the maker of evolution can be fully known and recognized for his efforts. ("For I have created him for my glory," Isaiah 43:7)

This anti-entropy principle means that both upward and downward movemens will continue as they began. According to Newton's law of inertia, objects in motion will continue in the same direction unless acted upon by an external force. The upward path of evolution needs no adjustment—it has already been acted upon by the external force of transcendental inspiration, even if this has been unconscious. The individual on the downward-moving path, who is losing what he has to the anti-entropy principle, is at some point the beneficiary of the external force—on the basis of Grace: He finally has to see himself. This is the third awakening that awaits everyone. It is the turnaround point from which we rise and get on the evolutionary side of the law of inertia.

The Dual Self

As we may awaken from a pain in the body during sleep, we awaken on the spiritual path from the pain of our inner division, regardless of our level of evolution. Like Dante at the beginning of the *Divine Comedy* we awaken in a dark wood—the darkness we stumbled into by being asleep. At that point we may realize that our limitations and our ignorance are not things that can be shaken off or blinked away but instead are quite resistantly interwoven with the totality of who we are. This thing that was mysteriously there when we awoke and refuses to go away is the one thing—because of its unnaturalness, indeed its unreality—that we can't forget about. Like the pebble in our shoe that insists on being noticed, it is always there to bedevil our hopes for happiness, purity and achievement—attributes that we sense, on an even deeper level of the mind, are our birthright.

But this very awareness of our negativity—which is the meeting point between our higher consciousness and the incredible imposter within—is the beginning of the process of liberation. This awareness is forced upon us as the path out of the dark wood. The moment that we subject the "bad self" to consciousness, it starts to fade—simply because it's an illusion.

Thus we already hold the key to the door in the wall, to "the narrow way which leadeth unto life," (Matt. 7:14)

While studying for a Master's degree in the Science of Creative Intelligence at Maharishi University of Management in the late 1990s, I came across the statement in Maharishi's book, *The Science of Being and Art of Living*: "Human life is a mixture of good and bad." Now everyone knows that human life is a mixture of good and bad. I myself had been knowing it every day since I started Transcendental Meditation many years previous. But precisely because it is such a common understanding, his words had the effect, not of teaching me something exactly, but of making me know that I knew. It was the kind of experience that, as Shelley said of the art of poetry, makes us imagine what we already know. It brought the knowledge into another level of resolution, and the important point became not the particular constitution of human life but the principle of good and bad itself.

An analysis of this principle reveals the fundamental nature of human life to be neither good nor bad but something beyond both. As with the opposites daylight and darkness (discussed in Ch. 1) good and bad cause each other and thus have no fundamental reality. If the illusions of good and bad are the abiding constituents of relativity, then the ultimate reality of human life is Absolute. This is what logical dualism can't see; and if we have trouble seeing it, logical dualism is the reason.

When the "bad self" sprang into being, what was left became "good." What hides behind this duality has neither of these limitations. The good/bad relativity that clouds our mind is the dark wood that envelops us. It is no accident that in the Divine Comedy Dante chose a dark forest as the place of awakening. Nor is it an accident that in the Vedas human life is called the forest of illusion, sangsara, and that sangsara is called the human mind.

The Oneness of the Self, the infinite Good, is not attainable without a human body. Spiritual liberation can come only from human bondage and only from increasingly subtle awareness of that bondage. Only by looking at current reality is it possible to see the ultimate; for the latter is just the former seen clearly. Nature is a good Mother. By showing us the deficient and the partial she guides us to become perfect and complete. If we let her, she will re-condition (uncondition) us for life in the cosmos. She knows that the happiness of her children resides finally in their ability to see and to know, that the bliss of the Self will be made manifest by looking, and that the world we now think is different from ourselves will be revealed as our own.

To look at the self, even the negative side, is most natural to the species, if not to modern man. The more imbalance there is, the greater is the priority for self-referral. It is as natural as an animal curling up within itself when it is sick. We saw earlier that through the limitations of our awareness the many are brought forth from the singularity of sanghitā. Correspondingly, by our conscious attention the many are returned to the One. To apply the Self to the self is the only true healing technique. It is part of the self-sufficiency Mother gave us, that we left in the psychiatrist's office.

This is seeing and knowing. By seeing our limitations we know them and immediately, in the deep mind, currents move to alter the surface waves of thought and behavior. This natural self-referral process also brings to mind rules of right behavior we have acquired from external sources or that have arisen from our conscience. Seeing and knowing are raised to the pinnacle of their healing power by the infusion of transcendental consciousness into the thinking mind through regular practice of Maharishi's meditation. As the practice furthers, the self is seen more clearly, and more transcendental knowledge is at one's disposal.

Awareness of a fault with desire to change it spontaneously initiates remedial action. Knowing what is wrong is a concept that elicits infusions of Being from a level much deeper than the intellect. From the desire to change, the healing process moves inexorably to conclusion. However, as salutary thoughts rise into the thinking mind and are acted upon, the intellect becomes involved. Without the intellect's participation we would never have a clear idea of what has occurred and thus could not ascend to the next obstacle to development. At this point, the intellect is able to attach concepts and words to the changes we are experiencing. From a concept remedial action has occurred, and from that action the intellect alights on a concept.

We have discussed how the intellect (reason) thinks it knows everything. In this case, as soon as it notices improvement of a fault or the removal of an obstacle it decides that it caused those changes. It thinks it has figured out the problem and solved it. This is what most of us do constantly. But in effect we are overcoming the problem in the intellect after intuitive knowing has already taken care of it. As Bob Dylan sang:

> Genghis Khan and his brother Don
> Could not keep on keepin' on.
> We climb that hill after it's gone,
> After we're way past it.

The trouble with this is that it leads to the habit of deciding what specific changes we want and what form we want the changes to take. This may be good in the short run, but over time it is bound to interfere with the healing power of Nature. Maharishi says, "Nature knows best how to organize." We are applying the finite mind to the problem when we could be employing Nature's omniscience. When we relax in the trust of God's "mysterious way," the mind remains innocent and ready to accept the natural changes that are coming. The human organism heals itself beginning with the spontaneous act of noticing something wrong.

Maharishi has never used the terms seeing and knowing that know of, because through the regular experience of transcendental consciousness we become increasingly aware of ourselves spontaneously. However, seeing and knowing are the natural results of the growth of transcendental consciousness. They are terms I have given to this process.

The Negative Self

The term "bad self" comes easily when we are talking about that part of us that won't behave as we want it to. It amply covers all our contradictions. But with its corollary, the "good self," we have divided into two what is really one, as well as implied the necessity of eliminating half of what we are. The compulsion to excise the bad self is like signing up for a lobotomy—it contains things we will need when we are alright again. For example, a concert pianist may discover that his excessive emotions are causing behaviors that interfere with his work. But he is a musician in the first place because of his emotional sensitivity. What is weakest in one now will become his greatest strength. Under stress a bone breaks at its weakest point which, when mended, becomes the strongest.

The negative self is inevitable because we are born with both good and bad tendencies. Free will, by which our negativity can be overcome, is of marginal use to most of us because it is usually overruled by past negative karma. Free will becomes more useful as consciousness evolves, and indeed with Self-realization, is identical to the Cosmic will. The Cosmic will is ultimately our own by our unity with God in Self-realization.

Our personal evolution is as inevitable as our negativity. Evolution causes expansion of consciousness by neutralizing wrong tendencies, and this occurs through the on-going elimination of stress in the nervous system. This natural purging (unstressing in the body) may temporarily upset the mind and cause more wrong action. Thus some expression of negativity in action is for most of us a virtual inevitability set in motion by the positive force of evolution and the stress release it produces. All progress means eliminating the negative as well as taking on the positive.

Of course, our wrong actions must be paid for reciprocally (as we will discuss in the next chapter). But this doesn't mean they are necessarily "bad." The Seven Cardinal Sins of Christianity are not taught as something bad to be eliminated but as a distortion of something good to be moderated: The Sin of pride is a distortion of good self-image, of lust a distortion of love.

The force of evolution that ultimately overcomes wrong action has maximum power when transcendental consciousness is being experienced on a daily basis. And the unstressing, because it takes place at a quiet, deep level of the mind, is experienced only as passing thoughts.

In Vedanta and Yoga the terms most often applied to the negative self are "ignorance" and "bondage"—ignorance of Reality and bondage to our past karma. These are probably the most comprehensive terms for our current condition vis-à-vis Enlightenment. Certainly they are the most accurate with respect to their opposites—knowledge and freedom—that characterize that blessed state.

Bondage and ignorance cloud the mind and, as the ultimate cause of all the darkness that besets us, they blind us even to the extent of our ignorance. Observe a five-year-old with its mother in the waiting room. Aren't its mood swings from laughter to tears, contentment to fretfulness, hyperactivity to torpor, cooperation to rebelliousness those that still stalk our days, perhaps minus the tears? When we are young we think we will outgrow our faults. But what appears to be confirmation of this in later life is often only habituation to them, control of them, learning to cope. Of course we improve but, without regular transcendence, improvement is by soul-time which is much longer than body-time. We don't "put away childish things" nearly as readily as we think. We believe age will quieten the passions, but in *The Crestjewel of Discrimination*, Shankara writes of an old man creeping along on his quivering cane, "and his body is still full of desire." Even such a personage as St. Paul said, "What I would, that I do not; but what I hate, that I do" (Rom. 7:15).

To get a picture of our negative self we need only make a list of what we despise. If "all love is love of the Self," as Maharishi says, then all hatred is ultimately self-hatred. What we love in people and things in general are their manifestations of the naturally lovable Absolute Self—beauty, truth, Reality. We love in a personal way when the particular positive manifestations are those we share. Likewise, we recoil from things that deny the Self—discord, violence, falsehood. We particularly despise those negative manifestations that we share or formerly shared—like the ex-smoker who can't stand the sight of a lighted cigarette.

Anger is another of the Seven Cardinal Sins. Anger arises when an external force blocks an intention or interferes with a positive mood. Those sensitive souls who regard anger as their most uncomfortable emotion will find comfort in Lord Krishna's words in Ch. 3, v. 37 of the *Gita*, and Maharishi's comment. Krishna says, "Know [anger]...all consuming and most evil... to be the enemy here on earth." Maharishi comments:

> When the flow of a...desire is obstructed by another flow, energy is produced at the point of collision, and this flares up as anger, which disturbs, confuses and destroys the harmony and smooth flow of the desire. Thus confusion is created in the manifested field of Reality, *and the very purpose of manifestation, which is the expansion of happiness, is marred; the very purpose of creation is thwarted* [emphasis added]...[Anger] is like a fire which burns up everything in its path....That is why

anger is called "the enemy" by the Lord.
(Maharishi has often repeated that the expansion of happiness is the purpose of creation.)

The ultimate remedy for anger is development of the state of consciousness that is uninvolved with the relative field of existence. Suppressing, or trying to suppress, anger is not an issue in that state because the anger we might give vent to does not touch the uninvolved Self. Maharishi is said to sometimes get angry. (Those who have experienced this directed at them say is it extremely cleansing. It seems to burn out the fault, oversight, or ignorance that elicited the anger.) But this occurs in the relative field only. Maharishi (the Self) is not touched by the anger. In the state of Self-realization, "anger" is only the impersonal response of Nature to a violation of it laws.

We find ourselves naturally freer of anger as consciousness expands. In fact, a good way of measuring our self-development is that anger is less violent and thus has less effect on us and on the other person.

By Maharishi's comment above we see that anger can result from a desire to succeed or achieve. He has said that the expression of anger should be avoided because it pollutes the environment. If we are unable to avoid this expression, a step in the right direction is to *see* it and know—as in Maharishi's case—that it is not *me* who is angry, and to realize that the anger is being progressively moderated by this observation.

We have seen that the breakdown of the wholeness sanghitā is conceptual, not actual. Nonetheless, we fully partake in it and thus bring forth the negative self which causes us to misperceive everything. A grid is laid over our vision, as it were, which divides the wholeness of life into seemingly unrelated fragments.

The primary illusory duality is life and death. Despite the blissful and illuminating near-death experiences (or death-return experiences) that have come out in the last couple of decades—

and despite everyone's best intuition that life continues "in a better place"—fear of death continues to consume us. Freud said it is the basis of all other fears. Yet it is seems certain that, to the tranquil soul, the transition is no greater than from youth to age—requiring only a change of bodies that the *Bhagavad-Gita* likens to a change of clothes: "As a man casting off worn-out garments takes others that are new, so the dweller in the body casting off worn-out bodies takes others that are new." Death is an illusory phenomenon based on point of view like a ship's disappearance over the horizon while voyaging on unchanged.

From boyhood on, Alfred (Lord) Tennyson experienced transports of "boundless being" that he considered "the only true self," states of awareness that were far from confusing but "the clearest of the clear, the surest of the sure, utterly beyond words—where death was almost a laughable impossibility." Perhaps it is because the physical apparatus ceases to function in such an immediate and final way, while only the unseen spirit goes on, that our intuition in the matter is overcome—or at leased caused "grave" doubts. In any case, death (as extinction of individuality and consciousness) is the Big Lie that robs of us an essential truth—that of our immortality. It rivets our attention on a single detail of life's great tapestry and blinds us to the whole that constitutes our freedom and peace of mind.

Most of us live in a state of chronic discomfort of which we are not clearly aware for lack of any real contentment to compare it to. This is not very different from knowing we are alive only by our pain. Sometimes we tell ourselves that everything is alright and resolve to lay down our striving, only to wake up to a feeling of guilt more painful than the struggle.

Our confusion would not be so tragic were it not for the soaring freedom promised by the human organism created in the image of God to live in infinite bliss. Fundamentally we are not born merely to have a vision of the whole, but to be it. This is our birthright; yet we are the only species not living according to the design of its organism. Humans were born to evolve; this is our distinction and our sorrow. We have given the term "human" to ourselves, but higher intelligence must see us more like a God-animal. Born to be gods, we are merely scattered fragments without the realization of it, often behaving worse than a lesser thing that is whole. Because of our confusion we are more confused than we can know. In most cases, without the illusion of wholeness provided by the self-reflective, surface mind (see "The Third Awakening") our error would crush us. By the merciful laws governing consciousness, we learn the real extent of our ignorance only gradually, only as increased stability and a more mature understanding allow us to endure it.

Animals cannot violate the Natural Law so they don't suffer (though they do feel pain). We on the other hand can't seem to comply with Natural Law, and this is why we suffer. To stray from the blueprint of life, from the knowledge of how to live that is encoded in our souls, is to suffer. Around the time of the Renaissance, Natural Law, often rightly regarded as the law of God, was understood as a built-in guide for all success and happiness both inner and outer. But since industrialism's subjugation of Nature (in which material desires became law instead) the real law has virtually vanished from human thought. It is now honored mostly in the breach, as the unknown cause of suffering that seems to strike at random. Thus we labor without the benefit of this infallible, invincible and blissful standard of right and wrong that is our very Self.

Maharishi says, "The realized man is awake in the light of the Self, while the ignorant is awake in the light of the senses." In every case, whenever our ignorance and bondage rise up to create obstacles, our hyper-enlarged senses are the cause. Whether it is a false belief in our maturity, our petty hatreds, the fear of death, or our violations of Natural Law, it is the senses's domination of the mind that leads us astray—toward the very opposite of Reality. In *Dark Night of the Soul*, St. John of the Cross says:

> Oh, miserable is the fortune of our life, which is lived in such great peril and wherein it is so difficult to find the truth! For that which is [in reality] most clear and true is to us most dark and doubtful....And that which gives the greatest light and satisfaction to our eyes we embrace and pursue, though it be the worst thing for us, and make us fall at every step.... And if he is to know with certainty by what road he travels, he must perforce keep his eyes closed and walk in darkness, that he may be secure from the enemies that inhabit his own house—that is, his *senses and faculties* [emphasis added].

In Ch. 2, v. 67 of the *Gita*, Krishna tells Arjuna: "When a man's mind is governed by any of the wandering senses, his intellect is carried away by it as a ship by wind on water." Maharishi comments:

> The mind by nature thirsts for greater happiness. Let us suppose it is enjoying experience through a particular sense. In its eagerness to enjoy the utmost that sense can provide, it becomes absorbed in the process of enjoying, and in this one-sided absorption loses the power of discrimination, which is the main faculty of the intellect. This is what the Lord means when He said the senses rob a man of intellect.

It's one thing to understand in the abstract that society is blind. But it may be quite another thing for a man to realize that, as Bob Dylan sang, "His brain has been mismanaged with great skill." The British novelist E. M. Forester said, "Life is a public performance on the violin in which we must learn the instrument as we go along." Many of us can identify with this. The real pathos, however, is that each of us believes he is making music. And the situation reaches its full tragic absurdity when one comes to realize that even the best music played on the scale of dualism can only lead us further into error. At the end of the day, our best members turn out to be those who, like Socrates, can say only that their distinction over other men is, "I know that I don't know."

Consciousness of the Unconscious

Expansion of consciousness is the reduction of the unconscious. The spiritual life is essentially a process of turning the unconscious mind into consciousness. Freud "discovered" the unconscious mind, and even today we consider it a given in life. But to Maharishi it owes its existence solely to our ignorance and bondage, two disabilities that clearly limit conscious. Certainly, the unconscious must be replaced by consciousness if Self-illumination is a fully conscious state.

The unpredictable nature of the unconscious mind has troubled man forever—long before we thought in terms of a conscious and an unconscious. On the one hand it is unknown, dark and terrible. On the other it provides the inspirations and intuitions that cause us to rise above ourselves and approach our divinity. It also contains urges to animal wildness and self-destruction. But the only thing wrong with the unconscious is the two little letters un. All of its terror and fear fade when it becomes conscious. The deep urges whose ambiguous messages have led us into wrong action begin to come into accord with Natural Law.

Like all processes, this begins slowly and picks up speed as it furthers. The unevolved mind may respond negatively to a stimulus to the unconsciousness, such as a full moon, but evolved spiritualists know that the full moon heightens intuition. The terror of the unconscious mind and its paradoxical transcendent beauty will continue to trouble man as long as that region is not brought into awareness. The horror behind the curtain is the curtain itself.

The two forces of the unconscious, while they are a unity

deep in the mind, express themselves as disconnected urges of "good" and "bad," neither of which by itself is Reality. In *Howard's End* E.M. Forster says,

> We are meaningless fragments, half monks, have beasts, disconnected arches that have never joined into a man…. Only connect!…Only connect the prose and the passion, and both will be exalted and human love will be seen at its height. Live in fragments no longer. Only connect the beast and the monk and both, robbed of the isolation that is life to either, will die.

In the *Phaedrus* Plato sets up a metaphor for the journey of the soul that involves a chariot drawn by a white horse (reason) that is noble and easily guided, and a black horse (unconscious passions) that is lumbering, shag-eared, deaf and unyielding to whip and spur. This horse rushes forward heedlessly to enjoy and beget at the sight of beauty while the white horse wants to just stand in amazed rapture of it, as does the charioteer. This conflict is intrinsic to the ordinary mind, and if it never comes to the surface to be resolved (i.e., if it remains under control) it either tears us apart or brings us to a state of exhaustion. The black horse is too strong to be controlled by the white one, but will never be controlled without it. The only way that reason can gain its rightful position of leadership over passion is to rise to the level of the power of transcendental reason in the light of the fully conscious mind.

Later, in the *Symposium* (as Genevieve Lloyd explains in *The Man of Reason*), Plato "saw passionate love and desire [the black horse] as the beginning of the soul's process of liberation through knowledge; although it must first transcend its preoccupation with mere bodily beauty, moving through a succession of stages to love of the eternal forms."

Lloyd says that Diotima, Socrates's instructor in the art of love, presents the art "as a progression, moving from love of the particular to love of the general, and [later] ascending from earthly beauty….But in Diotima's version of the lover's progress, reason does not simply shed the perturbations of passion, but assimilates their energizing force." Through transcendental experience, reason becomes passionate and passion reasonable.

Progress along the continuum from appreciation of human beauty to transcendental beauty is the natural growth of life we are all undergoing. This progress, says Annie Besant in *The Ancient Wisdom*, inevitably involves "impacts" to the soul which may include wild passion and sometimes even the perpetration of lethal violence. ("The moral sense in man is the duty we have to pay on mortal sense of beauty"—Vladimir Nabokov.) But these impacts, which are the virtually inevitable result of our past karma, are merely the first lurching charges of the beast down the long road of excess that will wind up at the palace of wisdom.

Chapter 5

The Path up the Hill

"Midway upon the journey of our life I found myself lost in a dark wood, where the right way was lost. Ah! How hard a thing it is to tell what this wild and rough and difficult wood was, which in thought renews my fear! So bitter it was that death is little more." So begins the *Divine Comedy*, which Dante just called the *Comedy*.

The first word of the great epic poem names the symbolic point in life in which we awaken to higher purpose. In a larger sense it indicates the farthest point on the great circular (or spiral) journey of the soul, covering many lifetimes, at which its outward or material work (technically called "evolution") is mostly done, and it turns in the inward direction for Home (involution). The dark wood, by literary consensus, represents the forest of sense. Dante also equates it with mortality, referring to it as the "pass which never left person alive." This echoes the Garden of Eden story, where wrong use of the senses (eating the fruit) is likened to death. And this death is of course nothing but banishment to the world we live in.

In front of him offering a means of escape Dante spies a hill, which represents the "true course of life." He soon meets the shade of the Latin poet Virgil (Dante's idol) who refers to it as "the delectable mountain which is the source and cause of all joy." But Dante's way is blocked by three ravenous beasts-

-a leopard, a lion and a she-wolf. These once-real beasts now symbolize lust, pride and avarice—creations of our own mind. They are so horrific that Dante cannot proceed, and Virgil proposes to be his guide around the cosmos through hell and purgatory and so arrive at the Heavenly Realm.

The Divine Comedy owes its genius in part to characterization of human life as a flight from "all joy" into hell—through fear of self-created illusions. But because the obstacles *are* illusions and not objective phenomena, the ability to go straight up the hill lies in our consciousness. So let's suppose for a moment that in the author's imagination he had taken the inner path up the hill, the direct route to God. The great poem would not exist. This alternative throws into clear relief our personal trip around the cosmos through hellish agonies and painful purgings; that is, it doesn't exist except as we imagine it. Our life is a self-authored comedy, a magnificently elaborated drama based on perception of our error as real. The path up the hill is the one that everyone eventually takes—the journey from illusion to Reality.

Dante's narrator is unable to say how he entered the dark wood, "so full was I of slumber at that moment when I abandoned the true way." Likewise if we had been awake to our errors in the past we wouldn't be hostage to ourselves now. It is our past karma that stymies us. It's barks and growls exhort us to face what we have sown in order to free ourselves from it. They are there merely to inform us that we are now awake to our illusions and can therefore no longer justify running from them.

What if Dante's character hadn't been so eager to quit the scene? Perhaps he would have learned that it is possible to make friends with the beasts. Maybe they were hungry only for the sweets of his attention. If so, he would have discovered a means to control them. An illusion is the last thing one can safely ignore. Being a creature of his own mind, it exists precisely because he has ignored it. It thrives on denial. To discount it is to give it strength. The more we run from it the more it imperils us. There is an African folk tale of a pride of lions that positioned the old toothless lions in a certain area of the forest to roar loudly when they saw a gazelle. The frightened animal would run the other way—straight into the jaws of the young lions. The only way to deal with a dreaded illusion is to "run to the roar."

What is happening in our lives now is virtually inevitable by karmic law because we planted the seeds. Some came up as peach trees and some as nettles. We can only be free of them by self-acceptance. "In the face of the inevitable," Maharishi says, "the only course of action is acceptance." Natural law requires that we accept karmic inevitabilities because we are their cause. "As ye sow, so must you reap." Being created in the image of God means that *cause* falls within our consciousness—our current day-to-day consciousness as well as our eventual co-creatorship as God-conscious beings.

Never feel Guilty

Our unwillingness, our inability, to take the straight path up the hill is a vestige of primal fear. Even though the beasts that once chased us into caves are now metaphors for the psychic weakness that characterizes modern life, they are no less terrifying. This weakness, referred to as "the loss of personal power" by Carlos Castaneda, is bound to bring guilt; for unconsciously we know we are running from ourselves.

Maharishi said, "Never feel guilty even though you are." Maharishi often proves that brevity is the soul of wit. This statement contains a great truth about our dual nature. It is a reference to the hemispheres of the brain and teaches that we must use both of them to overcome a fault. That is, we must know our guilt (through the left-brain of reason) and yet not blame ourselves (through the intuition of the right-brain). If we remain ignorant of our wrongdoing or deny it, we will only commit further violations of Natural Law and create more suffering; but if knowledge of our culpability turns into blame, we can lose the spontaneity of action necessary for growth. Rationality knows our guilt, but hasn't the scope to see the real cause. Thus it makes itself the cause and can advise only more will power as the solution. But this is bound to fail because the ultimate cause is not in the wrong action itself but in the past karma that caused it. Behavior altered by reason alone cannot affect this cause. It's "best laid plans" are forever laid waste by the gales of emotion and the hurricanes of deep need. Ultimately, thought and action are brought fully into accord with Natural Law only through Pure Consciousness, which Maharishi refers to as the "Home of all the Laws of Nature."

Practically speaking, then, our day-to-day behavior is not so much led by a moral ideal as pushed along by our past karma. The politics of self is the art of the possible. Certainly we must ultimately measure ourselves against an ideal, but that comes only from knowing who we ultimately are and does not involve attempts to change ourselves. Real improvement comes only through the non-rational mind, which must be opened before we can enter the all-healing Pure Consciousness. The modern poet Robert Bly said that real growth takes place only in ritual time; that is, when reason is suspended.

To seek an external ideal while neglecting self-development and self-knowledge is the kind of cart-before-the-horse approach that characterizes modern religion. But seeking the end of the rainbow without knowing where we are now can lead to wrong turns. And if we find the pot of gold without knowing who we are, who has found what? The stigma against self-knowledge thrives on the permissiveness of our era, which encourages us to deal with our vices by calling them virtues. We are also overwhelmed by modern business whose vast resources are used to get us to cover our discontent with material things.

But the negative self must be seen if it is to be healed. At the level of development of most of us, if we are not conflicted, we are fooling ourselves. There must be the spur of a contradiction between who we are now and who we are in Reality if the Pure Consciousness that ultimately rectifies the situation is to be brought to bear. Blessed are those who find the Cross they are to bear in this life. And twice blessed are those who are able to re-shoulder it each time they fall. It's not how many times we fall that counts, but how many times we get up. In the spiritual game one doesn't lose until he quits.

If we have done something we wish we hadn't, like lying to a friend to protect ourselves or violating one of our sacred personal rules, we are poised to sink into guilt. While recognizing that we have hurt someone, if we regard our act as karmically inevitable (or at least beyond our ability to control) and refuse to blame ourselves, there has been no error in the larger sense. ("Beloved, if our heart condemn us not, then have we confidence toward God," 1 Jn. 3:21). The fact is that in the degree we have realized Pure Consciousness, we are not to blame, because to that same degree the eternal forgiveness of God has intervened between the act and the blame. Self-blame is alien to the soul, as is any other sin. Although we must reciprocally reap the wrong action we have sown, it doesn't have to injure us. Maharishi likens the karmic discharge of wrong action to a man who borrowed a thousand dollars and became a millionaire before the loan was due. The payback must still be made but it doesn't touch him.

Blame is also our usual response toward others when we think they have wronged us. To blame is to judge, and we know not to judge lest we be judged ourselves. But non-judgement, like charity, begins at home. By not judging ourselves we learn not to judge others.

Understanding these things, refusal to heap blame on ourselves is the furthest thing from the self-deception it might seem to be. It is a clearly conscious forebearance based on knowledge of the nature of consciousnesss. It comes from searching the conscience, not ignoring it—from a cleansing rather than a covering up. Nor does considering our wrong action inevitable lead to more wrong action—that would be logical, but it is not the way the mind works. We can be regretful without adding the emotional burden of self-blame. If we continually blame ourselves, as most of us have done since the moment of our rude awakening, we will never overcome the damaged sense of self-worth that causes us err again and again. Self-blame is eliminated before wrong action.

The karma of past lives holds controlling interest in the corporation of self. We have discussed how God and our past karma function as the same thing in establishing our tendencies in this life (Ch. 4, "The Third Awakening"). The world was written by the Hand of God in invisible ink, as it were, which our lives are merely a tracing over in the belief that we are the author. Omar Khyyam wrote:

> With earth's first clay they did the last man knead,
> And then of the last harvest sowed the seed,
> And the first day of creation wrote
> What the last dawn of reckoning shall read.

Mythology East and West

In the 1970s someone in Maharishi's movement came up with a wire recording of the voice of his master, which was probably made in the 1940s or '50s when Swami Brahmananda Saraswati was the Shankaracharya of Northern India. It was scratchy in places but the few words were clear. Guru Dev said, "There are four million kinds of lives a soul can gather. To get a human body is a rare thing. Better make full use of it. Otherwise you are selling a diamond at the price of spinach." There was a long silence followed by loud crackling and then the voice said, "Never think of yourself as a weak or fallen creature."

The final words are similar to Maharishi's teaching on guilt. If Maharishi didn't learn the general concept at the feet of his master, it is in any case natural to the Eastern hemisphere of the brain. It is also just possible that Guru Dev, expecting that the recording would find its way to the West, chose words that would counteract the doctrine of original sin, since this is so damaging to spiritual progress. The two opposing views on this question arise from the distinction between Western and Eastern creation mythologies, which diverge sharply at the very foundation of the world.

In Judeo-Christian mythology man is separate from God —a separateness that extends into the afterlife where, although one may be with him in Paradise, unity is achieved only by Special Grace. God formed man from the dust of the ground and breathed into him the breath of life—meaninig that from the beginning, man was "other." As a result although man toils through his life with the availability of God's help, his closeness to God is built upon effort over historical time. In Judaism this is effected by covenants in which God promises to protect if man promises to obey.

In the mythology of the East, God creates man from his own being; that is, turns himself into man. Man doesn't have to struggle for unity with God, for he was never separate. He must only realize this unity by discovering the essence of himself. (There is one instance in Christianity where a man was created on this Eastern model. This is what is meant by "begotten, not made" in the Nicene Creed. Jesus came from God and was God. Unfortunately, he was the only one to come into being in this fashion, his own teachings notwithstanding.)

The essential difference in man (and all of creation) East and West is a reflection of the essential difference in God East and West. In Hinduism, Buddhism, Taoism and Zen, as well as in the Vedas, God is primarily impersonal—a transcendental, absolute unity of universal opposites, which is the nature of man. (Personal gods may be many and varied, especially in Hinduism, but they are all understood to be merely aspects of the one transcendental Brahm.)

In Judaism, Christianity and Islam the impersonal God is rarely considered. Thus in the Western religions being made in God's image does not include a transcendent aspect. Man's soul is immanent in the world but can never be simultaneously transcendental to it like its Eastern counterpart. Man cannot transcend the world except by death. He is bound to it without the capacity to experience unboundedness. This contrasts with Maharishi's statement that, "The nature of man is the boundless within boundaries." This is what gives life its bliss. Without the resistance of the water, we couldn't have the joy of swimming.

God made man however he did, either from the dust of the ground or from something else. But by the power of myth to determine belief, Jews, Christians and Muslims must struggle to overcome their separateness from God. We are separate, then, because we think we are; whereas, Hindus of all stripes live and die in fundamental unity. We get what our belief system allows us to expect. There is a parable in Sufism (the mystical form of Islam) of a man being shown around heaven by God. He sees a man on a couch eating luscious fruits and surrounded by beautiful dancing girls. "Is this all there is?" the visitor cries in disbelief. God says, "That's all he wanted." As the psychologist William James said, "The final measure of a man is his vision."

These creation myths East and West reflect the characteristics of the right and left hemispheres of the brain respectively. As we have seen, the right brain is holistic and inclusive, the left dualistic and exclusive. In the East man is already a member of the club, maybe just a little behind in his dues. In the West he is still waiting to be admitted. He doesn't realize that his admittance is based on nothing but an right-brain-style acceptance of himself; and he can't accept himself as he is. He must reinvent himself first, through surface-mind management of his moral behavior. And he doesn't know that this is not the member's key.

Mark Twain said that when you come to the Pearly Gates, make sure your dog hasn't followed you. He won't get in. Entrance is based on favor, not merit. If it were the other way around, the dog would get in and you'd be out.

We are favored because we have consciousness—the Godlikeness that no other species has.

The God most of us have created for ourselves is all good; and in thinking of ourselves as different from that, there is a tendency to believe we must be bad. Our left-brain mentality sees God as a man in the sky who looks a little like Charlton Heston in *The Ten Commandments*, a God who thinks according to logic, and therefore vengeance. We allow ourselves to be driven to become better by threats of eternal damnation. Yet our negative self, with its A-to-Z list of errors, is not a matter of morality, but of knowledge. It results not from evil but from ignorance.

Action, Impression, Desire

The inevitability of our violations of Natural Law can be understood as a mechanical process—a cycle of action-impression-desire—as explained by Maharishi. All actions good or bad leave impressions that are stored at the deepest level of the mind, the soul, and are the only things we take with us from this life. This is the karma that characterizes our next lifetime. But in our current life as well, the impressions rise to the surface as desires to repeat the actions that caused them—even (especially) illicit actions that we found pleasurable. Once these desires get up a head of steam they are much too much to be resisted by reason. Thus the cycles repeat themselves over and over, perhaps through lifetimes, until consciousness evolves enough to neutralize the desires and prevent wrong action.

It is the natural weakness of reason vis-a-vis emotion that makes wrong action practically inevitable. Although we have a free-will choice in the actions we take, this will almost always give way to a strong desire, or habitual need. However, the will can reassert itself by understanding why we are thus compelled. We can go straight up the hill of life, like the little engine that could, if we cause ourselves, by knowledge, to think we can.

We begin to take control of our inner beasts and pacify them with our attention. They become acceptable because everything is acceptable on the basis of self-acceptance. ("All things are lawful unto me," said St. Paul, 1 Cor. 6:12.) When this dawns on us, we turn for Home. We have followed Dante and Virgil partway around the cosmos numberless times after slumberous awakenings, but this time we made the hairpin curve we couldn't negotiate before and take the road less traveled. We leave behind the story of humanity that Dante so clearly read, and write a new chapter in the Garden of Forked Paths.

Chapter 6

Escape and Denial Behaviors

Ignoring, denying, and trying to escape from our inner conflicts are responses we have learned from society which, particularly in America, must always put on a happy face. But by accepting our imperfections—accepting ourselves as we are—the war within us begins to subside and happiness starts to take its place.

It is possible to ignore our limitations to such an extent that we never know they are self-caused. The ordinary man blames others and circumstances for his problems, but even among spiritualists this old habit of the rational mind dies hard. In the final analysis we run from the roar because we don't hear it within us.

One of our escape mechanisms is hurry. Hurrying paves over the difficulties we encounter in daily living, and in the process obscures the experiences that are so important in learning how to live.

Hurrying to Trouble

The fast pace of modern life hides the fact that hurry is basically a phenomenon of consciousness not invented by the present era. Spiritualists long ago recognized it as our most graceless rejection of the God-given beauty of the present moment. In his Meditation Manual, Ram Das mentions Abby Dorotheus, the director of a seventh-century European nunnery, who counseled her charges that nothing was important enough to disturb themselves with hurry. In effect, she was counseling patience long before St. Teresa of Avila instructed her nuns similarily in sixteenth-century Spain:

> Let nothing disturb you,
> Nothing frighten you;
> All things are passing,
> God never changes.
> Patience obtains all things.
> Nothing is lacking to him who has God.
> God alone suffices.

Patience is not merely forebearance in the hope that something good will happen; it is a technique to draw the desired thing to us. Seeing our hurry is the beginning of patience. It settles and expands the mind so we see things more clearly and make better decisions. As an antidote for hurry, patience opens the mind to receive what we want and need.

The quiet, expanded state of consciousness we are seeking is shattered by the starter's gun of hurry. The goals that can be achieved by hurry are not where Being is leading us. They are not the achievements of thought and action based on Being. They are not the spiritualist's goals, which all center on ease, non-involvement and enjoyment.

When we feel the impulse to hurry it is because of some ill ease, and we are bound to take steps to change it. We can either speed up or slow down. Naturally the temptation will be to get the job done as quickly as possible. But if we take this course we will barely experience anything between there and the completion of the task, much less enjoy it. Nevertheless, we hurry because slowing down frustrates the logical mind. If, on the other hand, we work easy instead of hard, we take advantage of Maharishi's delightful counsel, "Life should be lived like we're on vacation." Slowing down changes consciousness and thus changes external conditions. It shifts conditions to a ballpark outside the field of logic. Instead of struggling for the result, we work for the enjoyment of the action.

It would be difficult to over-emphasize the damaging influence of the chronic hurry that besets our society. Maharishi, except for advising us to meditate every morning and evening, makes only two rules. One is not to do anything we know to be wrong. The other is, "take it easy during the day." To Maharishi, taking it easy is serious business. In his commentary to Ch. 6, v. 1 of the *Bhagavad-Gita* he says that "Being...becomes permanent...in the nature of the mind...in the whole field of thought, speech and action, in the whole field of man's life...by the practice of Transcendental Meditation *followed by activity that is unforced and without strain* [emphasis added]". It turns out there's a close relationship between taking it easy and not doing what we know is wrong: Violation of Natural Law, wrong doing, occurs most often when we are hurried or anxious, because the big picture is reduced to a detail of self-interest.

Hurry and struggle succeed each other. We get caught up in this cycle by believing that a certain material accomplishment is higher priority than maintaining the Self, which obtains all things spontaneously. (God alone suffices.) When material effort goes beyond what we can maintain with easiness, strain is caused, and external achievement ceases to be consistent with inner growth. Hurry is always hurrying to problems.

In more cases than we realize, hurry becomes an addiction we pursue for its own sake. It becomes strain for the purpose of strain, because the second incident covers the uncomfortable effects of the first. It has been said that "heat doesn't wait for the sun in order to be hot;" it creates that agency. Like this, our predispostion to hurry creates a situation in which it can express itself.

Easiness during the day is a reflection of the silence of Absolute Being. The habit of being innocently mindful of when we are starting to hurry (*seeing*) opens up ever-deeper levels of easiness in which the physiology becomes increasingly more settled. Life is lived with more deliberation, creativity, enjoyment and progress. Things are appreciated in their finer values. Taking it easy comes from transcendental consciousness and leads to transcendental consciousness, where perfect silence comes to coexist permanently with dynamic action.

Action for its Own Sake

The habit of hurry makes us work only for results and ignore the possibility of enjoying the actions that lead to them. In Ch. 2, v. 47 of the *Gita* Lord Krishna tells Arjuna: "You have control over the action alone, never over its fruits. Live not for the fruits of action." The meaning here, Maharishi explains, is that one should focus only on the actions so that the whole mind is brought to bear on the outcome.

> It would be absurd to infer from this verse that a man has no right to the fruits of his action....The doer has every right to enjoy the fruits....[but] he should fulfill the action with such complete devotion and undivided attention that he is oblivious even of its fruits. Only in this way will he achieve the maximum results from what he does.

The quality of the result can be only according to the quality of the action. Therefore, by hurrying through our daily tasks in expectation of the fruits, we miss both the material fulfillment and the enjoyment of the doing. Getting there is not just half the fun, it's all the fun. As Goethe said, "The deed is everything. The glory nothing."

The surest and most complete way to fulfill this ideal is to find work that is in accord with our dharma. The Sanskrit word dharma has two meanings, cosmic and individual. It is the cosmic righteousness that upholds evolution by keeping a balance between the fundamental forces of creation, maintenance and dissolution. It is also the kind of daily occupation that upholds individual evolution. One's dharma is ones natural vocation, his calling, the work for which he was born. Working in our dharma keeps us easy and settled so that we avoid stress in the joy of the actions.

Dharma is vitally important in the Vedic scheme of things. Maharishi comments on Krishna's statement in Ch. 3, v. 8 of the *Gita*: "Do your allotted duty [your dharma]."

> An important aspect of natural duty is that it is imperative for a man; if he does not perform his allotted duty, he will be engaging in actions which lie outside the path of his own evolution.
>
> Allotted duty comprises all the actions which enable a man to survive and evolve. The rightness of such actions lies in this: that in performing them a man feels no strain; they are not a burden in life; in one stroke they maintain life and lead to evolution....
>
> The question arises of finding out what is one's allotted duty. In those parts of the world where natural divisions of society still exist, a man's duty is apparent by virtue of his birth in a particular family....But in the complexities of the mixed civilizations and mixture of traditions in the world today, it seems hard to discover one's "allotted duty."

Maharishi says that meditation allows one to find his dharma.

> Meditation...smoothes the flow of life and naturally sets the stream of life in accordance with the laws of nature, upholding it on the way to higher evolution.

India's crumbling caste system is much maligned in today's world. But it was not the evil it is thought to be. It held life together and smoothed the path of evolution. A child grew up watching his father work at a trade or craft and had learned it naturally and completely by the time he was old enough to work. Compared to this, our modern methods of finding a job seem like shooting in the dark. How often we miss the target is evident: From multi-national corporations down to the local convenience store, companies are filled with people working at jobs that hold no real interest for them. Job hatred is rampant and jokes about it fill the halls of every business. Boredom, incompetence, confusion and disorder reign at every level. Many people go through a succession of jobs that they tolerate only under the threat of poverty.

Failure on a job is most often a result of working outside one's dharma. This means you could be aiming too low as well as too high. Maharishi once said, "If you fail at something, try something higher." The German poet Rilke allowed that he had never succeeded at much in life but had failed at higher and higher things. We could end up winning the war after losing every battle. If you have trouble finding your dharma, ask yourself, "What would I do if I knew I wouldn't fail?"

The Vedic concept of dharma aims very high. In Ch. 3, verse 35 of the *Gita*, Krishna says, "Because one can perform it, one's own dharma, (though) lesser in merit, is better than the dharma of another. Better is death in one's own dharma: the dharma of another brings danger." Maharishi comments:

> It is evident from this that there is a yet greater danger to life than the phenomenon of death. Death as such only causes a temporary pause in the process of evolution. A pause like this is no real danger to life because, with a new body taken after the pause, more rapid progress of life's evolution becomes possible. A greater danger will be something that actually retards the process of evolution.

The Vedic scheme takes the importance of our life's work beyond the grave. In looking for work many people's only concern is in "keeping upset with the Joneses," to use Marshall

McLuhan's phrase. Some of them find jobs than are not only uncomfortable but dangerous.

We can fully understand the Hindu caste system only through the concepts of karma and reincarnation. One is born into a particular caste because of his karma, and by fulfilling its duties—which is considered worship of God—he is reborn into a higher cast; so that he goes from *sudra* (servant), to *vaishya* (farmer or merchant), to *kshatriya* (warrior and statesman), to *brahmin* (teacher of the Vedas). From here the soul gains liberation from the cycles of birth and death. The importance of duty is brought out in an ancient Indian folktale (from the *Panchatranta*).

A pious Brahmin went every morning to the Holy Ganges to bathe. One day he happened to have his hand outstretched when an eagle flying over dropped a little mouse into his palm. On his way home he thought, "My wife and I have no children; what if I turned this cute little mouse into a beautiful young woman whom we could marry off to a prince and thus provide for our old age?"

Lifelong devotion to Brahm had given the gentleman great powers, and no sooner had he had the thought than a lovely little girl of six appeared walking beside him. He presented the little girl to his wife and told her of his plan, to which she agreed.

When the gorgeous girl was of marriageable age, the Brahmin decided to marry her to no less a god than *Surya*, the sun. Surya appeared upon his command, and the girl said, "Oh, daddy, he's much to hot!"

"What is more powerful than you, O sungod?" the man asked.

"The wind," Surya replied. "It blows the clouds and hides me."

The Brahmin called the wind, whom his daughter pronounced "Too fickle."

"Who is more powerful than you?" The Brahmin asked.

"The mountain, for I must go around it."

When mountain appeared it answered that, "Mice are stronger than I because they eat me up from within."

So the Brahmin called a mouse, and as soon as it showed up, the girl fell in love immediately and cried, "Oh, Daddy, change me into a mouse so that I may marry and fulfill the duties of my kind."

Maharishi says that achievement comes not from hard work but from "desiring at the finest level." At the finest level of the mind, thought interfaces with cosmic dharma and thus gains infinite power to fulfill all desires and needs. This doesn't mean that one shouldn't work hard. It means that hard work becomes easy. Most of us would do better to look in our hearts to find a job rather than in the newspaper. There is something in here—and thus something out there—for everyone.

Charles A. Reich explains how society thwarts our built-in desire to work for the joy of it and exploits our proclivity to work for the fruits.

> We are trained to be aware of the goal of our actions but not to be aware of what is actually happening. In most cases to make our jobs palatable, our attention must be directed away from the actions to the reward. When we are asked what we do for a living, we answer, 'I am a lawyer. I help people and businesses to solve their problems. I help everybody to know the rules that we all have to live by and to get along according to these rules.' We never say, 'I struggle with crowds, traffic jams and parking problems for about an hour. I talk a great deal on the telephone to people I hardly know. I dictate to a secretary and then proofread what she types. I have all sorts of meetings with people I don't know very well or like very much. I eat lunch in a big hurry and can't remember what I've eaten. I hurry, hurry, hurry. I spend my time in very functional offices with very functional furniture and never look at

the weather or sky or people passing by. I talk but I don't sing or dance or touch people. I spend the last hour all alone struggling with crowds, traffic and parking'.

The complaint here is not against traffic jams, of course, but that our moment-to-moment activities are being denied by both society and ourselves. What is being denied is the content of our lives—the doing—the only thing that can make us happy. The form—"I am a lawyer, I make $250,000 a year"—is and should be incidental. When we don't remain conscious of our actions, the source of happiness is taken away and everything else crumbles. Maharishi says, "Gently resist the temptation to chase your dreams into the world. Attend to your inner health and happiness. Happiness radiates from you like the fragrance of a flower and draws all good things to you."

Denying Current Reality

Everyone feels that somehow the bad self should not be. Yes, but to try to leap over problems to the goal of liberation is to disregard the path we are own. Maharishi has often talked about this, saying that "the realities of the freeway are not the realities of home." It is a common desire of modern spiritualists to want to get home right now, and a lack of spiritual understanding causes them to create a false positivity. This can become chronic as more and more "spiritual excitements" (a contradiction in terms) are sought in order to avoid the discomfort they expect to feel (and therefore do feel) from living in the moment with simple awareness. Maharishi says, "When we live in the present, Nature organizes our destiny." Life can come to be built entirely on the illusion of "being there." One senses in modern spiritualists a disdain for even mentioning a bad self. This unnatural posturing creates inner turmoil and can lead to a greater need for falsely stimulated experiences.

All gains must be paid for reciprocally. In the story *The*

Monkey's Paw by W.W. Jacobs, a couple is given the paw of a monkey that will grant three wishes. The couple wishes for money. The next afternoon a man from the factory where their son was working comes to their door with an insurance check for the exact amount they wished for and tells them their son was caught in a machine and killed. In their anguish they wish their son back to life, but he is so grossly mangled and in such pain that they must use the third wish to send him back to rest.

Ignoring current reality in the quest for self-justifying spiritual experiences can easily turn into the "activity sickness" that is prevalent in all phases of modern life. In his theory of *divertissement*, Blaise Pascal, the seventeenth-century French philosopher, says that rest is man's highest good. All we do is done so we can rest. But then we find that our rest is beset by thoughts of all the evils that could befall us. Thus we are diverted, driven back into the activity which is both a blessing and a curse.

One of Dr. Chopra's cases (explained in *Unconditional Life*) shows how one may begin to deny his negativity. Dr. Chopra was seeing a patient who was trying to banish her fear of a recurrence of cancer by positive thoughts. "I have read so much about the damage you can do to your body with negative thoughts that I spent the whole year after my operation dreading the least sign of one," she said. Chopra's view was that many people, in their well-intentioned efforts to accentuate the positive, do not escape their problems but only increase them. They want to put an end to suffering but mistakenly choose the tactic of denying their true feelings. We all have hidden pain inside, he says, and trying to suppress it is not a virtue. It is only an impossibility.

"Does opposing your negative thoughts lessen their power?" Chopra asked his patient. "Doesn't it just delay the day when they will come out in one way or another? Think about it. You probably put in a lot of time not thinking negatively. It must require constant vigilance and effort on your part. Yet as soon as the pressure is off, don't these denied feelings rebound with double intensity?...Negative thoughts come on their own, even in the face of our strongest opposition. It's...something we have to accept."

It has been said that self-will is the only thing that burns in hell. But accepting ourself makes it easy to "let thy will be done." Our current reality is the Cross upon which we crucify self-will to liberate the spirit. What we do with consciousness at any moment determines our reality. Our past was also made up of moments, and in those moments when we acted in ignorance we incurred negative karma. But that karma as yet has so substance; it takes the form and power we give it right now by our knowledge and belief.

As we have seen (Ch 4, "The Third Awakening"), the destiny we are currently living through can be thought of as either the will of our past karma or the will of God. Accepting ourself intellectually is the beginning of re-destining our life. In terms of direct experience, transcendental consciousness is total self-acceptance and complete re-destination.

The Field Effect

It is generally conceded that pain comes from the attempt to avoid pain. That is, once it starts (by a predispostion to avoid it), it increases the more we struggle against it. Similarly, life's problems can only get worse when we strive with them. They cannot be lastingly solved on the level of consciousness where they arose.

The negative self will not be overcome by attempting to treat its parts individually. Our separate faults grow out of a field of consciousness that must be subsumed by a deeper field where they don't exist. Using mental effort against faults can be compared to struggling to bring to mind a name that is "on the tip of the tongue." And in both cases, only if consciousness is allowed to settle to a deeper level is the desired brought forth.

Maharishi says, "If a wrong man does something right, it turns out wrong; if a right man does something wrong it turns out right." The determining factor is the field, not the individual act. A healthy plant cannot grow from poor soil. If the terms "right" and "wrong" seem too vague, the conscience always distinguishes them clearly. A wrong man is one who is one who is not right with himself. He is uncomfortable, doesn't like himself, and when he looks in the mirror he doesn't like what he sees.

Funnily enough, a close examination of our positive and negative selves reveals that our negativity by itself is not the problem. All discomfort in life results from the conflict between the positive and negative selves. The Greek word *agonia*, from which we get our word "agony," means "conflict." If there were no negative self, or if there were no positive self, we would have no conflicts. (Dr. Chopra explains the mechanics of inner conflict by using the three gunas. If we are considering indulging ourselves by watching the late movie on TV, sattva-guna—the impulse to evolve—says we should go to bed. Tamas—the guna that limits or retards—says we should watch the movie. And rajas—the action guna—is urging us to make a decision.) Because of our positivity our negativity makes us unhappy. When the negative self suddenly sprang into being early in life, the good self arose with it. Thus the two are parts of the same field of duality.

The field effect of modern physics describes a condition in which superficial opposition (in this case, conflict) is found to be a unity on a subtler level of existence. Around the middle of the twentieth century, during the period when Einstein was attempting to postulate a Unified Field of Natural Law, the fundamental forces of Nature had been reduced to four: electromagnetism, the weak (extra-nuclear) force, the strong (intra-nuclear) force, and gravity. In 1967 Glashow, Salam and Weinberg unified the first two of these. The electromagnetic force and the weak force, now called "electro-weak", were found to be manifestations of an underlying field common to them both. Thus their respective particles, the electron and the neutrino, which have very different properties and behaviors, are now understood as essentially non-different, like two branches of a tree when they reach the trunk. When consciousness achieves the field that underlies the positive and the negative, duality and thus the conflict disappear. Put another way, both good and bad give way to the capital-G Good. This occurs in the ultimate field, the Transcendent. This is the field of which the Sufi poet Rumi spoke: "Out beyond ideas of right-doing and wrong-doing there is a field. I'll meet you there." Transcendental Pure Consciousness is, in fact, the ancient Vedic discovery of the Unified Field of Natural Law known to modern physics. The identity of the two has been proposed scientifically by physicists at Maharishi University of Management. Their inquiries were perhaps inspired by Maharishi's statement that "Nothing exists but the Unified Field." Reduced to their simplest form, these highly scientific proposals rest on the fact that the Unified Field (proven intellectually by objective science) and Pure Consciousness (directly experienced in the practices of Maharishi Vedic Science) are both known to be infinite; and there can be only one thing that is infinite.

What our consciousness experiences is our reality. The solution to problems, then, would be to experience life in expanded consciousness—to shift our awareness to a field where the problem doesn't exist, and ultimately to the field that is eternally problem-free. From this level arises Maharishi's statement: "The answer to every problem is that there is no problem." This shift involves using what he calls the Principle of the Second Element. "To struggle against problems," he says, "is by definition struggling in darkness." It is as if we are trying to read the directions and assemble the apparatus of our life in a dark room; when all that is needed is to turn on the light—to bring the second element. Problems are never lastingly solved on the level of the problem. In fact, strictly speaking, no problem is ever solved—only transcended.

Knowing that We Know

We have seen that refusing to look at our spiritual ignorance is a mistake that limits growth. In effect, it says to the face of existence, "I have no delusions, my concepts of the world are correct, I know what I am doing." Too often we believe this without question when in fact it is dead wrong, and will prove to be so when we hit the wall of reality and break down in rage or despair. Even after this, most of us blame the world.

It is better to be able to say, "I don't know," at those times when, in spite of our best intentions, our karma returns something we can't handle. Assuming that we know keeps us in a field where we don't. Knowing that we don't know takes us to a field where we can learn.

Socrates's statement, "I know that I don't know," declares a willingness to abandon one's direction when it turns out to be wrong, and thus to abandon an illusion. If we never have to say, "I don't know," we may be merrily cultivating our ignorance rather than weeding it out. The famous psychiatrist Carl Jung was treating a conventional young man who one day arrived for his appointment in high spirits, saying he'd just gotten a promotion at work. Jung looked at him with an ironic smile and said he'd be happier for him if he'd said he just got fired. ("There are more things in heaven and earth, O Horatio, than are dreamt of in your philosophies.")

To be willing to change our point of view is vital, particularly if we are seeking the spiritual rather than the material goal. Here, the whole game is to adjust ourselves according to the knocks of the world. The world is the guru. And like a guru, it opens our mind to infinite possibilities of knowing. Maharishi's meditation brings the ultimate field of consciousness into our vision, and with this we have a chance to surpass even Socrates. The Absolute lifts relative knowing—with its accompanying shadows of ignorance—into the bright light of certainty. One doesn't know everything, but everything his awareness touches is experienced at the ultimate, invariant level of Reality in which he can declare, "I know that I know."

Chapter 7

The Linch-pin of Acceptance

When we accept ourselves as an interwoven mixture of good and bad—instead of denying and trying to escape our negativity—consciousness changes, the field changes and our conditions change. Acceptance is life. We are children of the Most High God and have no more choice to refuse what comes to us, good and bad, than we had as infants to refuse what was offered by our most high parents.

When consciousness opens to our negativity, negativity opens to the healing power of consciousness. The quietest place in a hurricane is in the eye. Self-acceptance helps us move deep within the quiet center of consciousness around which everything swirls. If we hang back on the periphery we will forever be buffeted this way and that.

We chose what is happening to us in this life because we knew what we needed in order to learn and grow—and then we forgot it. There is a nursery story that the little cleft in the upper lip is where the angel pressed us to seal our lips. If we had access to that knowledge we could not grow into the actualization of it with the wonder and awe of life that Maharishi says is the highest human emotion, and which is openness to the continually arriving unknown. As it is, the knowledge is stored in our unconscious mind, and the expansion of consciousness that begins with the innocence of acceptance helps take us to the realization of it.

The importance of acceptance can easily be seen in a person who has a deformed body or some other serious handicap. Sometimes it is clear that the person has not accepted what he chose and is therefore holding himself back. This is not so easily noticed in the ordinary person who just has a lot of problems—except that his resentment, his anger, and the self-hatred he turns on others are of the same cause. But in both cases the discovery that there was a choice is critical—even if, because of past karma, it was the only choice.

In *The Gnostic Gospels* Jesus says, "You must learn to suffer in order to learn not to suffer." The subtle teaching here is that learning to suffer and liberation from suffering involve the same mode of consciousness. That is, acceptance of one's suffering—learning to suffer—is of the same mindset as acceptance of the bliss that follows from it. We will not be awake to the bliss if we are not open to the pain.

One learns to suffer not by denying it but by becoming uninvolved with it. These are very different things. Non-involvement is the style of consciousness in Enlightenment: One is not involved with the world and its suffering and thus is equipped, by the bliss and love that are his life, to help remove it. All the beauty in the world comes from the Uncreated—from the uninvolved transcendental consciousness that, with proper meditation, becomes the nature of the mind. The evil of the world, its ugliness, and our suffering response, is a result of our identification with it.

In Christ's teaching above, the *form* of the mind is the same in suffering and in bliss—openness, willing acceptance—but the *content* changes. This being the case, it is not suffering as an emotional experience that is being extolled but only the principle, or the form, of suffering. In fact, the emotional experience of suffering cannot turn into bliss until it begins to subside through acceptance, or begins to be replaced by the direct experience of Pure Consciousness.

Since we must deal with this unpleasant subject, a key in "learning to suffer"—in suffering gracefully and purposefully—is to realize that in reality what is happening is the only thing that can happen and that therefore there is no difference between what is and what should be.

In a lecture many years ago the chairman of the then-MIU physics department discussed the inevitability of what is: There is only one way a particle can manifest from the quantum wave function, and it is dependent on the type of observation of the physicist. Like this, situations take an inevitable form from the individual's observation of himself.

When this is clearly realized, the mind loses interest in searching for causes of his suffering and all the resentments this can produce. He naturally focuses deeply into the feeling of the pain and thus neutralizes it. The old self progressively gives way to one who knows how not to suffer.

Getting a Handle on Suffering

Ramana Maharishi, a South Indian Yogi of a generation ago, died of cancer. (It seems ironic that a fully realized being can die of such a common disease. It can only be that negative karma of past lives was being discharged, not karma of the present life.) Late one evening before Ramana's passing some of his disciples heard him in his room at the ashram screaming in pain. They came to see about him, and one of them lovingly reminded the master that he'd always said life is bliss. Ramana told them that he was in pain but not suffering. There is a crucial difference between these two. In the first case, one realizes that what is happening is the only thing that can happen; in the second, there is the inevitable "why me?" Animals don't suffer because they see no difference between what is and what should be. They have no consciousness of self. In the superconsciousness of saints like Ramana Maharishi, this principle has expanded to its fully opposite dimension: Individual consciousness has been subsumed in universal consciousness, and what is happening is known as the only thing that can happen.

The world-teacher J. Krishnamurti also experienced great pain without suffering. Mary Lutyens in her biography *The Years of Awakening* recounts how, late at night, she would hear the young man in his room crying out in pain, and then the next morning see him full of radiant energy as he started off on his walk before breakfast. One day she he asked him about it. He expressed the growing non-involvement of his consciousness with the world: "There is a lot of pain, but I'm not there."

In its essence, suffering is emotional involvement with not having what is desired; fulfillment is getting hold of the desired. Under the first condition, the act of acceptance temporarily compensates one for lack of experiential fulfillment. It provides us with the fulfilling knowledge that we are doing what is right and needful. Obeying the natural laws that govern liberation, in other words, becomes the source of enjoyment. ("For his delight is in the law of the Lord; and in his law doth he meditate day and night," Ps. 1:2.) And this mode of consciousness acts as a powerful vacuum to draw the desired to it. Knowing that we are doing what is needful is on the level of the intellect. But the intellect is only one of the complementary ways that acceptance begins to transform bondage into bliss.

The other way is direct experience. Acceptance is the form consciousness takes when it is at peace with itself and current reality; and if not at peace, this devotional acceptance contributes to bringing it about: The mind settles inward where it finds an ever-deeper intellectual understanding of the evolutionary value of acceptance while it directly experiences its ever-deeper rewards. In this whole-mind process, acceptance of the negative can grow to fullness and become all there is. When acceptance of our negativity (as the will of God or of our past karma) fills the mind completely, the resulting vacuum is infinite openness to positivity.

Acceptance of the whole of what we are—positive and negative—is essentially love of the self, self-affection. In this state we may sorrow for lack of what is desired, but as Father Felician said to Evangeline:

>…affection was never wasted.
> If it enrich not the heart of another,
> Its waters, returning back
> To their springs, like the rain,
> Shall find them full of refreshment;
> That which the fountain sends forth
> Returns again to the fountain.
> Patience; accomplish thy labor;
> Accomplish thy work of affection!
> Sorrow and silence are strong,
> And patient endurance of godlike.
> Therefore accomplish thy labor of love,
> Till the heart is made godlike,
> Purified, strengthened, perfected,
> And rendered more worth of heaven!

In Longfellow's exquisite poem, *Evangeline*, she has searched for years for the other side of herself, for Gabriel her displaced love, as we search for our better self. When advised to give up her painful yearning and settle for another—as we might be advised to give up the quest—she replies:

>I cannot!
> Whither my heart is gone,
> There follows my hand,
> And not elsewhere.
> For when the heart goes before,
> Like a lamp, and illumines the pathway,
> Many things are made clear,
> That else lie hidden in darkness.

As we have seen, the negative and positive selves arise simultaneously. That these two are the final measure of a human being is logical dualism. Dualism knows nothing but right-doing and wrong-doing, which succeed each other in on-going cycles and bind us to relativity—the gold chain and the iron chain. Our presumption to think only in terms of one or the other is the prison we find ourselves in, the Gate of a Thousand Sorrows that we have come to love. Duality is the canker at the core of human life, the illusion of all illusions that has been accepted unquestioningly for more generations than can be counted, and a profoundly debilitating disease that this present consciousness is powerless to heal even in the unlikely event that we know we have it.

Whether we like it or not we are infected with a lethal logic we can't root out. Nor can we live with it; for it separates us from the self-unity that the soul will never stop yearning for. This is a life-stopping problem. In Zen it has been likened to having a ball of burning lead stuck in the throat that we can neither spit out nor swallow. If we absorb it, it will kill us. But we can't expel it because it has become an inextricable part of us.

Under conditions like this, our only recourse is to declare the problem unreal. A choiceless situation cannot be foisted upon one who refuses to accept the terms. The answer to the problem is not in doing something but in knowing something; and this knowledge is the clear realization that what sticks in the craw of life is only a viewpoint, an opinion, a blind belief that has grown from the lifeless soil of duality, the most profound addiction man can fall prey to.

With this understanding, the handle to make the necessary change comes into our hand. It involves the everyday discontent we cannot escape. Our error is in accepting the ball of hot lead (duality) as real. This throws us into gridlock, making us think that we can somehow get rid of it all at once like a tumor, and yet being unable to act. The key to the world, then, is awareness of the discontent we experience every day, this moment. In this way, Nature organizes our destiny. This is "learning to suffer"; in Zen this takes the form of dispassioned observation of our plight. This is all but impossible without self-acceptance; but with self-acceptance, our consciousness begins to shift to another field. We can't remove the burning ball of logical dualism, but by seeing and knowing we can remove ourselves to a dimension where it doesn't exist.

The viewpointless viewpoint of transcendental consciousness is the mountaintop of self-observation, supreme in-the-moment living. As in the case of Krishnamurti, "not being there" is this transcendental non-involvement. For some, expanding the vision to an appreciation of the infinite greatness of the one Reality of God is the only way to come out of this suffering. The suffering that forces this vision upon us is often the last step to Enlightenment, as it was in the Book of Job.

The Lord said of Job "there is none like him in the earth, a perfect and upright man, one that feareth God, and escheweth evil" (Job 2:3). Because of his righteousness Job possessed such wealth of sons, daughters, and animals to make him "the greatest of all the men of the east" (1:3). However, through the sudden and radical purification of the nervous system that is sometimes necessary for the final extinction of ignorance in wise men, suffering came to Job. In the Biblical story this was the result of an agreement in which God allowed the devil to have his way with him. That God *allowed* this, is a mythological way of saying that Realtiy—that is, the *natural* order of things—was actually governing the process. Job, knowing that he had not sinned—not in the usual sense is the word—complains long and loud against his wretched suffering and the loss of all his possessions (also allowed by God). But when God shows Job His omnipotent and omniscient greatness, Job says, "I have heard of thee by the hearing of the ear, but now mine eye seeth thee, wherefore I abhor myself, and repent in dust and ashes" (42:5,6). And, in the end, when "the Lord gives Job twice as much as he had before" (42:10), this is also a metaphor for the spiritual and material abundance that naturally attend upon final purification of the nervous system and expansion of consciousness to Enlightenment. Job had to give up all his involvements with relativity, even his sons and daughters, in order to receive twice as much of everything on the basis of his non-involvement in the absolute greatness of God.

In the *Bhagavad-Gita*, Arjuna went through a process governed by the same principles. Like Job, he was the most evolved man of his time—again suggesting the darkness before the dawn of Self-illumination. Like Job, Arjuna regained all that had been taken from him—after the ferocious battle he was reluctant to undertake against his kinsmen. And, again like Job, Arjuna was blessed with a vision of God.

In the eleventh chapter of the *Bhagavad-Gita*, "The Vision of the Universal Form," (translated here by Annie Besant), Arjuna "beheld the whole universe, divided into manifold parts, standing in the one body of the Deity of Deities." Within this form he saw all the gods including the Creator, Brahmā. "By thee alone," Arjuna says,

> Are filled the earth, the heavens, and all the regions that are stretched between. The triple worlds sink down, O mighty One, before Thine awful manifest Form....Like Time's destroying flames I see thy teeth, upstanding, spread within thy expanded jaws. Naught know I anywhere, no shelter find, mercy, O God! Refuge of all the worlds! I worship thee! Have mercy, God supreme!

God said to Job, "Deck thyself now with majesty and excellency; and array thyself with glory and beauty [and] cast abroad the rage of thy wrath: and behold every one that is proud, and abase him." Similarly, Krishna says to Arjuna,

> Time I am, laying desolate the world,
> Made manifest on earth to slay mankind!
> Not one of these warriors ranged for strife

Escapeth death; thou shalt alone survive.
Therefore stand up! Win for thyself renown,
Conquer thy foes, enjoy the wealth-filled realm,
By Me they are already overcome,
Be thou the outward cause, the left-handed one.

Because of the lack of mythology in the *Bhagavad-Gita* there is a certain difference between Arjuna and Job: Arjuna's suffering (his *agonia*, or conflict) comes not from "on high" but from an inner inability to reconcile the dictates of heart and mind. He is torn between the love of his kinsmen (even though they have usurped his throne) and his bounden duty as a warrior, as a member of the kshatriya caste. Inability to reconcile heart and mind is the central problem all of us face in life; it is the central theme of the *Gita*, the element that still gives it currency after 5,000 years.

Natural Law

Our happiness and achievement in all areas of life are determined by whether we obey Natural Law or violate it. When we act in accordance with Natural Law we are blessed with its bounty. "The entire kingdom is placed at the disposal of the man who does the wishes of the king," Maharishi says. He has spoken many times of the "support of Nature" that fulfills life when we support Nature. We become Nature's agent for good in the world when we act in accordance with its laws, and that goodness blesses first the one who acts as the conduit.

Natural Law governs everything in the cosmos from the behavior of minute subatomic particles—which arise spontaneously from the quantum vacuum state of transcendental consciousness (the "Home of Natural Law")—to the thunderous activity of the great galaxies in space. Natural Law lays down the rules for successful human interaction, such as the Golden Rule—do unto others as you would have them do unto you.

If we follow Nature's blueprint, we build the Kingdom on an unshakable foundation. To the extent we deviate from the plans, we reap the whirlwind.

The oldest natural law on the books is, "Whatsoever a man soweth, that shall he also reap" (Gal. 6:7). This is the fundamental law of human activity, the law that the natural mind will take as its first priority, because violation of it can threaten our very survival. In our past there have been violations of Natural Law and we are reaping what we have sown. This harvest is the raw material of our bondage and, for aware people, can be the starting point of the spiritual life. The limitations we are subjected to are the lessons we have chosen to learn. And accepting the limitations is learning the lessons. Accepting the limitations imposed by our previous thought and action is to alter our future. It also alters our past because it roasts the seeds of potential bad karma that otherwise would have sprouted.

All feelings of discomfort or discontent, regardless of the specific cause, result from fulfillment being thwarted, which usually seems to come from an external cause. But everyone senses that life's obstacles have no real existence because time and a change of mind (a change of field) can render them impotent. Even the obstacle of our own death is a matter of perception, as Christ realized in his person, and St. Francis understood ("In dying we are born into eternal life.") Thus it is absurd to try to deal with problems as manifest symptoms except in ways that also deal with the cause—our consciousness and perception.

Not all problems are easily recognizable as illusions that yield to a change in perception. However, even the most blatant of them will prove to involve things we need to learn on the path, and in that sense will respond to a change of field. Suppose I come home late one night and the dog I recently acquired won't let me in the house. It takes great imagination to see this as an illusion. Yet if instead of responding with frustration and anger, I take the problem as my next lesson, I will see that over-coming it involves a change in my consciousness. Very likely I have come home in a rough, stressed-out mood and the dog has sniffed it. If so, the immediate response of accepting the situation could be enough to reduce the bad vibrations and restore the animal's peace. By the time I get in the house I will have changed my original perception of the situation, and the situation will have changed. I will see that the reality of the obstacle depended entirely upon my consciousness. This is a practical application of a verse from the Upanishads and of Maharishi's teaching that "In the presence of Yoga [self-unity], negative tendencies are neutralized."

The self-observation required of us here carries over to other situations and begins to pacify and expand consciousness, preparing it to eventually enjoy all experiences of life free of the dualities of attachment and aversion. These two conditions are commonly thought to provide the spice of life. But when they disappear into each other, what is left is happiness uncon-ditional. A great comfort can descend upon the mind when we are forced to see that the only way out is in. It may be experienced as a warm feeling of sweet sadness in which the sadness comes from dying to the old self and the sweetness is the reaching of a new heart toward God.

It is stress and not our natural mind that makes us want to fight the problem, draw our sword against an illusion. A favorite ploy of stress (like that of the its old-world equivalent, the devil) is to prick and probe at the frustration to make it worse, because the more evil I can impute to the external situation, or the more blame I can heap on the other person, the less respon-sibility I must take upon myself. Anyone can contrast the feeling that this attitude produces with that of the sweetness of humility. When we know that we are the cause, all obliga-tion to act against the oppression is removed, and the healing power of God becomes all the greater. To surrender on these occasions as a habit of life is to increasingly give more power to God and thus to make ourselves devotees of an ever-greater and more wish-yielding God. In terms of Vedanta, this process is explained as simply a shifting of our energy from illusions to reality.

When we encounter an obstacle to our desires, acceptance results in a physiological change that is the counterpart of the psychological change. This helps neutralize stress and makes it increasingly easier to accept future obstacles. Acceptance is taking the road of Natural Law to circumvent problems. Whenever we join forces with Natural Law we are always led upward and out of difficulties.

Resist Not Evil

When we resist evil it conquers us; by humility we become invincible. Paramanhansa Yogananda spoke of a man who never learned humility and was thus humiliated all his life. There is a Japanese saying that if two people have a confrontation, the one who backs down first wins. And Christ said, "Agree with thine adversary quickly, whiles thou art in the way with him; lest at anytime the adversary deliver thee to the judge...and thou be cast into prison," (Matt. 5:25). If we resist the violence done to us in a personal confrontation, we only provide motivation for further violence. If we hold our peace, we hold up a mirror in which the perpetrator sees only himself and his violence. The *Udanavarga*, an early Zen work, says, "He who feels no ill will pacifies those who hate. [The presence of Yoga.] To those who are good [to me] I am good; and to those who are not good [to me] I am also good; and thus [all] get to be good."

But the principle of "resist not evil" can be used in a more immediate way in confrontations between our positive and negative selves. If we don't struggle against our wrong tendencies, we don't stir our past bad karma into manifestation. We can also think of our negativity as a quicksand into which we can only sink deeper when we resist.

Christ's non-resistance of evil was based on his acceptance of others' actions in the ocean of his love. (Indeed, his love was so great that there was never any question of resistance.) We use the potential of love we have within us when we don't fight ourselves. But Christ's acts of mercy were also based on knowledge of our frailties. And we employ this other face of love when we replace self-struggle with seeing and knowing. (We saw in Ch. 4, "The Dual Self," that mere employment of this technique improves thought and behavior.)

We have seen that our actions leave impressions deep in the mind that surface as desires to repeat those actions (Ch. 5, "Action, Impression, Desire"). It's common experience that wrong desires are hard to resist because resistance causes us to want the thing even more. As in dealing with violence toward us, discussed above, when we resist our "evil" desires they are further stimulated; whereas, self-acceptance tends to neutralize them. It's easier to work the good stuff in than to try to work the bad stuff out. A lifetime of struggling with ourselves has left most of us trapped in the brambles of desire. This is often more than the human can deal with. It's what a man faces in life and what defeats him. He doesn't have a chance to die to his old self before it kills him.

All love is love of the self/Self. If we can love our own imperfections we can love anyone's. This is easier if we have an understanding of the perfection of the fully realized state. Its immaculate purity, power and freedom remind us that this is our Real Self, not this jumble of contradictions. It also reminds us that others are the same. The Indian *namaste* (the palms-together bow) is to be accompanied by the thought, "I bow to the God within you."

Stress, Consciousness and Enlightenment

Mere mindfulness that the long-time sun is shining behind the clouds of ignorance begins to endow us with an integrity, or mental coherence, which extends to the physiology and neutralizes stress. Internal coherence operates like the Meisner Effect in physics, which Maharishi is fond of citing as analogous to the self-protective effects of the inner unity that is Yoga. A magnetized iron bar, in which the wave motions of the electrons line up in order (called coherence) will spontaneously resist the passage (intrusion) of an electric current. In a piece of iron without this coherence, outside influences enter without resistance. It is coherence in consciousness that excludes disturbing influences coming from the physiology and the environment.

In the Vedas this effect is called *cavach*, of which there are numerous examples in spiritual literature. In the lions' den, Daniel's purity and peace placed him in a field of consciousness unapproachable by violence. Likewise with Shadrak, Meshak and Obednigo in the furnace. In the *Tao Te Ching*, Lao-tze speaks of a man whose virtue leaves no place for a charging rhinoceros to lodge its horn.

The highest spiritual significance of acceptance is that it functions as sacrifice. Acceptance of limitations on one's power as a human being is significant self-sacrifice. Renouncing the power of the senses and mind for a higher purpose is the central thesis of San Juan de la Cruz in *Dark Night of the Soul*: The night (the renunciation) of sense is the light of the soul; the night of the soul is the light of God. This is the real meaning of the word sacrifice—to "make sacred." The same renunciation is available to anyone: In the Transcendent, the self is sacrificed and Pure Being takes its place.

Beneficial physiological effects (settling down) accompany the mental effects of self-acceptance. Consciousness and the physiology, mind and matter, are subtle and gross levels of the same thing. The degree of imperfection in the physiology—stress—determines the extent to which we can express Pure Consciousness, and our level of consciousness determines how much stress we have. The totality of our bondage can be understood as resulting from stress because that is what limits our expression of Pure Consciousness. In the today's world, the supernatural cause of human error (the devil) is being supplanted by the concept of stress. One of Maharishi's contributions to modern spirituality has been to relate human limitation to something that everyone can relate to.

Maharishi defines stress as any influence in the physiology that limits consciousness, impedes evolution. Stress is most often caused by emotional or mental strain but can also be caused chemically (eating or drinking something damaging) and by physical trauma. Stress is deposited in the nervous system only—not in the mind; although of course it influences the mind directly. Neutralization of stress (purification) and expansion of consciousness happen at the same time. Maharishi's genius is in reducing the struggle for Enlightenment to one simple matter: a natural mental technique, practiced regularly, that goes deep enough to eliminate all stress. He says, "It is my joy to make things simple."

He also explains that the physical, mental or emotional discomfort we may feel at any time during the day is caused by the neutralization, the elimination of stress. Negativity is not entering the system, it is being expelled. The neutralization of stress involves some degree of reorientation of stressed organs or nerve tissues in the direction of their original natural functioning. These movements in sensitive areas of the physiology can cause subtle disturbances in our thoughts and feelings and leave us temporarily off balance. When this mood passes with the stess release that caused it, consciousness makes an evolutionary surge. If the stress release is very deep, it may be accompanied by a temporary physical sensation.

It is the natural tendency of the physiology to throw off elements that limit consciousness (which happens regularly in sleep and causes dreaming). Thus Maharishi continually emphasizes that it is the natural tendency of consciousness to expand.

Stress may not be noticed when it is being incurred, but only when it is being neutralized. We don't feel the pain of a sunburn, for example, until the body later starts to fight against the injurious influence. We may not realize we have strained ourselves until activity settles down and the stress starts to be released. Maximum stress is released in Transcendental Meditation because maximum rest is provided. But here, stress release is generally noticeable only as passing thoughts because the senses are withdrawn as the mind settles to deep levels.

Stress may be thought of as a shadow field that invades the mind-body as the cause of all discomfort and disease ("almost all disease," Maharish says, as do most physicians). Stress entered the system through our past wrong action. Our past violations of Natural Law, being unnatural, caused strain and put a crimp in our nervous system, limiting consciousness.

(This past wrong action is karmically caused, as we have discussed, and is closely related to our conditioning. That is, the constitution of one's karma causes him to take birth to a specific set of parents in a particular time and place needful for his evolution, and therefore determines how he is conditioned. In turn, our conditioning determines the type of stress we are subject to and the unique challenges we face.)

Although the stressed self, caused by negative karma, is essentially only a potentiality it is, practically speaking, as inevitable as our past. It has become the warp and woof of our consciousness. Escape and denial behaviors are the psychological equivalent of trying to excise the bad self like a tumor. The problems that make up our negative self are "particles" of ignorance embedded in the stress field and can be lastingly eliminated only by changing the field.

Maharishi speaks of "averting the danger that has not yet come:" Transcending thought not only neutralizes existing stress but creates the physiological coherence that prevents or limits its future invasions and future problems.

Consciousness and Conditions

The *Bhagavad-Gita* (the Song of God) is one chapter in the great epic poem the *Mahabharata*, about a ruling family of India, the Pandavas. It is the story of the Enlightenment of one man (Arjuna) through the words of the man/God Krishna. As we have seen, Arjuna, leader of the Pandavas and the greatest archer of his time, is a man of very high consciousness who nevertheless cannot see through the final duality: reconciliation of the dictates of heart and mind. This reconciliation is what removes the final obstacles on the path to Enlightenment.

In the first chapter of the *Gita* Arjuna lays out the problem that has resulted in his despondency. He sees before him ready for battle the usurpers of his throne—grandfathers, teachers, sons, grandsons—and is moved to "extreme compassion....I see adverse omens," he tells Krishna,

> nor can I see good from killing my kinsmen in battle....I desire not victory....Those for whose sake we desire a kingdom, enjoyments and comforts are here on the battlefield...these I do not wish to kill—though killed myself—for the sake of sovereignty of the three worlds, how much less for this world....Only sin would come upon us through killing these aggressors...how should we not know to turn away from sin we who clearly see the wrong in bringing destruction upon the family.

In the last verse of the chapter Arjuna, "having spoken this at the time of battle, casting away arrow and bow, sat down on the seat of the chariot, his mind overwhelmed with sorrow." His heart was full of love and his mind was clear, alert and full of purpose. Yet he was in a state of suspension because heart and mind were not unified. To bring about this unity—that is, to educate Arjuna fully—is Lord Krishna's purpose in the Gita.

Arjuna's compassion shows his fundamental goodness. But goodness, as the opposite of evil, is not good enough for Krishna. Arjuna has failed to see something, and it's not the problem, which he sees with a clarity that equals his compassion. He has failed to see that what he faces are not objective conditions but a reflection of his own heart/mind dilemma—a reflection, that is, of his consciousness. Accordingly, when Krishna begins his teaching (in Chapter 2, verse 2) he says nothing about anything Arjuna has said. Instead he says, "Whence has this blemish, alien to honorable men, causing disgrace and opposed to heaven, come upon you, Arjuna, at this untimely hour?"

Speaking thus, Krishna indicates that problems are not solved on the level of the problem," Maharishi says in his commentary:

> Analyzing a problem to find its solution is like trying to restore freshness to a leaf by treating the leaf itself, whereas the solution lies in watering the root....He [Lord Krishna] simply dismisses everything that Arjuna has said without analyzing it, because by analyzing each statement it would be impossible to resolve the situation. All problems of life arise from some weakness in the mind. All weakness of mind is due to the mind's ignorance of its own essential nature, which is universal and the source of infinite energy and intelligence. This ignorance of one's own self is the basis of all problems, sufferings and shortcomings in life. In order to root out any problem of life it is only necessary to be brought out of ignorance, to be brought to knowledge.

In terms of the physiology, to be brought out of ignorance means to be brought out of stress, because elimination of stress raises consciousness and gives knowledge of the Self. The physiological settling that accompanies self-acceptance allows increasingly more personal peace and thus allows us to know ourselves on increasingly deeper levels of our being. Changes in consciousness and concomitant changes in external conditions result from this.

In the books by Carlos Castaneda, his mentor Don Juan, says, "a warrior [a man of knowledge] is one who knows he can't change himself but tries anyway." We get the truth of this if we understand that the impossibility of changing ourselves refers only to the present level of consciousness. "Trying anyway" means the intent to change, not effortful struggle for something that he has, after all, decided is impossible. This intent is what changes the field of consciousness and makes the impossible possible. Sufficient intent can arise only from sufficient knowledge of our conditions. Indeed, clear awareness of our bondage and how it is compromising our life is that higher knowledge. And we can avoid knowing these things only by an unnatural rejection of the experiences, thoughts, and feelings that the self offers us. It offers these to us as our first priority, self-knowledge being the key to all happiness and achievement. In practice, knowing that we can't change ourselves means knowing that conditions do not change by treating symptoms. Working on the parts is doomed to failure from the beginning; whereas, expansion of consciousness ultimately makes failure impossible. Lasting external achievement results only from expanded consciousness and, since raising consciousness is effortless through proper meditation, there is nothing that we must do to achieve what we want in life. In fact there is nothing in this world that we can do. Seeing and knowing are reflections of the Enlightened consciousness that is out of this world.

It is not playing with words to say that you can change yourself only when you realize you can't. The ordinary man regards acceptance of his ignorance as a cop out and a prescription for failure. But our faults and problems leave us only when we realize they are inevitable and permanent. This idea is the utter antithesis of logic; in fact it is nonsense. And that is its value—it breaks the boundaries of the logical mind where the faults and problems have grown, and brings us to an impasse. And in this state of suspension we are able to see that only in the logical mind are problems permanent. In one form or another, this conviction is what leads one to seek self-improvement in transcendence.

This is seeing the big picture. But it requires seeing with the heart, not the head. If we step back from ourselves and look at our ravaged environment dispassionately, we will see it as a parallel case. There is a relationship between our body and the earth body (which the Greeks called *Gaia*, earth mother) which suggests a single solution. The damages visited upon our environment are like those caused by stress in our body, which results in our personal problems and faults. We have to consider these, like stress, as inevitable and permanent at the current level of collective consciousness. They are unavoidable epiphenomena issuing from the underlying consciousness of the civilization. If we see them only as a result of individual choices, we will be forever seeking individual solutions (watering the leaf) and lose sight of the field effect, where the real solution lies. Like the problems in our physiology, current environmental problems are not tragedies but phases in a long growth process. They are tragedies only when we look at earth-time through the eyes of our much shorter body time. The earth will eventually eat every building, freeway, mall and theme park—like it is right now eating Mayan pyramids—as collective consciousness changes. "A thousand years a city, a thousand years a forest." Environmental disorder and individual physiological disorder are greater and lesser degrees of the same problem. The organic approach to bringing about global environmental change starts when we understand our own individual problems as arising from a specific state of consciousness. This approach begins to take effect when we raise our individual level of consciousness; for the collective consciousness can be nothing but a collection of individual consciousnesses. "To make a forest green," Maharishi says, "it is necessary to make each tree individually green."

Enlightenment is the ultimate change of consciousness that changes all conditions—sometimes in surprising ways and always in superrational ways. Zen and Taoism are famous for paradoxical statements which obscure the relationship between consciousness and conditions that the student is presumably supposed to intuit. In the *Tao Te Ching* we find this: "The sage puts his own person last, and yet is found in the foremost place." What is the connection here? It is a state of higher consciousness. In putting his own person last, the wise man reduces his small self to the vanishing point and dons infinitude, rising to the "foremost place." The first part of the statement indicates a change in consciousness and the second part, the resultant change in conditions. "He treats his own person as if it were foreign to him," (meaning that he has transcended the mind/body) "and yet that person is preserved;" that is, he is beyond the decay of matter. "Is it not because he has no personal and private ends"—because he has transcended individuality—"that therefore such ends are realized?"—i.e., that he is in receipt of the bounty of Nature. "He is free of display," (being totally absorbed in God), "and therefore he shines," (in Glory).

In the 1970s the leader of the Movement in the United States was an outspoken individual named Jerry Jarvis. Teachers of Transcendental Meditation used to swap stories about his directness. In one of these, Jerry was lecturing to a large audience in New York City. He was asked what happens when you meditate. Jerry said, "Nothing happens when you meditate." Several teachers on the stage, hoping to instruct people from this audience, slunk down in their chairs. Then Jerry said, "But it will be the most significant experience of your life."

"Nothing" (no-thing) is the non-material "place" where we stand, like Archimedes, for perfect leverage on the world. In actuality, Transcendental Meditation does nothing. It is of no more value than the ground you don't step on when you walk across the lawn.

Don Juan also told Carlos that there is nothing a man of knowledge must do. That is, ever-expanding external achievement is made spontaneous by gaining full support of the irrestable flow of Nature. Floating down river in a boat, one does nothing while making maximum progress.

Krishna explains this in terms of the mechanics of consciousness (*Gita*, Ch. 5, v. 8,9):

> One who is in Union with the Divine and who knows the Truth will maintain, 'I do not act all.' In seeing, hearing, touching, smelling, eating, walking, sleeping, breathing, speaking, letting go, seizing and even in opening and closing the eyes, he holds simply that the senses act among the objects of sense.'

This is because, as we mentioned earlier, the Absolute (the Divine) is ever separate from and uninvolved with the flux of relativity. Maharishi comments:

> 'I do not act at all:' It is not that he holds on to this thought artificially but that the very structure of his mind is based on this natural non-attachment....He acts and experiences, making use of his senses, but within himself he is fixed in Being....He lives twofold: the stability of changeless Being constitutes the inner core of his life, and on the periphery is found the activity of the sensory level—the senses engaged in the experience of their objects.

We see that Maharishi has emphasized that this non-attachment is not a mood of the mind but its natural state when established in transcendental consciousness. However, we can get a taste of it in daily activity by remaining in the eye of the hurricane, the stillest place amid the storm of problematical sensory activity swirling around us. This is the daily consciousness that begins to change conditions.

Chapter 8

Self-observation and the Self-referral Life

In one wide-eyed glance of disbelief we saw the whole of our potential negativity become real. By the steady, dispassionate gaze of knowledge we watch it return to the illusion it always was.

Knowing beyond doubt that our past violations of Natural Law have produced a state of life divorced from Reality starts the process of leaving it behind. This has been our thesis concerning the negative self. We have said that our conditions in life are a result of our consciousness and cannot therefore be lastingly changed except through a change in consciousness. Acceptance of our error initiates that change. It allows consciousness to lay down the struggle against itself and take up its most potent weapon of all—intent.

There is a story in the *Puranas* (the aspect of Vedic literature that recounts the exploits of Enlightened beings of the past) in which Indra looses 10,000 arrows from his bow at once—by the mere intention to do so. The story brings to light what we could call the Principle of Full Intent—the power of intention as a separate human ability distinct from any doing, a power that can accomplish all doing. On the foundation of fill intent, the function of consciousness vis-à-vis error becomes merely silent observation and knowing.

By seeing and knowing, consciousness develops under-standing and love. These are the primary qualities that were lost in the stress resulting from our violations of Natural Law. Thus our error is structured in their opposites: ignorance and hostility. Mere witnessing is the most effective solution to the problems of the self because it brings the all-positive qualities of Pure Consciousness to bear on the self directly, unmixed with human concepts. This is the healing power of Self-referral, Krishna's administration of creation. (See Chapter Two.)

The Self-referral Maharishi is talking about here is not concentration or rigid focus. That kind of attention divides the mind and makes daily tasks more difficult. It also applies only limited power to the problem of self, not the full, transforming power of Pure Consciousness. Measurement theory in modern physics says that the observer influences what is observed. (We have seen that the physicist's observation causes the electron to manifest.) One of Maharishi's most important observations is that attention to any negative aspect of life will cause it to improve. The well-known Hawthorne Effect, in which observers merely watched factory workers perform their tasks, improved work. Self-awareness must be applied naturally. It must come spontaneously from the conviction of knowledge. If it is natural it will flow from the back of the mind and subtly influence all we do during the day—like always knowing we have our keys in our pocket.

It is very important that self-observation be entirely natural. We have talked a lot about seeing and knowing, but we don't want to get involved with it throughout the day. We tap into our reservoir of seeing ourselves only when we notice some-thing amiss in thought or behavior.

The Italian thinker Benedetto Croce has a unique view-point on the power of perception and self-observation. All knowledge whether of an event, an object, a concept or another person involves perception. In his pioneering work, *Aesthetic,*

Croce speaks of perceptual knowledge (which he calls by the technical term "intuition") as, in part, a process of freeing the individual from limitations. He says that perception, or intuition, is the process of giving form to the amorphous impressions and sensations we experience in daily life, like capturing the content of our lives in a succession of picture frames the way a movie director may look at a scene through his upraised hands. Croce calls this intuition an act of the human spirit. That is, it creates objective knowledge and at the same time removes us from it and makes us superior to it. It doesn't matter what the impressions or sensations are; it is by the interest they hold for us that they are given form. This interest, of course, represents who we fundamentally are. Thus, the intuition that gives form to vague impressions—that clarifies them and removes them from us—is an act of our fundamental nature, the spirit.

Croce says intuition also includes the expression of the formed impressions, and that the more care one gives to the expression the more free he becomes of it. The more consciousness one gives to the expression, in other words, the more that expression takes on a life of its own. If it is a personal problem or a destructive habit, it will tend to break up and disperse. If it is a beautiful theory or an artistic creation, it will leave the mind free to entertain others like it with a fresh spirit.

Keeping our life's perceptions in a frame of consciousness rather than obscuring consiousnses by our perceptions, develops naturally as consciousness expands. It is the difference between living in light and living in darkness. It means having control of life rather than being controlled by it. If our consciousness is swallowed up in living we have no direction home. To observe life dispassionately is to keep a picture of it in the golden frame of consciousness, to set it off in beauty, to view the world from a state of freedom the way Pure Consciousness views the universe framed in its unboundedness.

Maharishi has provided meditators with a self-observation technique to use outside of meditation for dealing with any pain or unwanted sensation in the body. One sits and closes the eyes and innocently (neutrally) feels the pain. This small amount of rest coupled with the attention of the mind provides an opportunity for the physiological activity of stress neutralization to complete itself and subside. Conscious neutrality allows the healing power of Pure Consciousness into the body unimpeded by attachment or aversion, and awareness expands to a field beyond that in which the pain was felt. Psychological and physiological discomfort is desolved in a field of higher reality. The elimination of the negative self is simply an experience of a deeper field. Our body is subject to a thousand ills that never see the light of day because consciousness is awake on a level of reality deeper than they are operating. The constant remission of cancer cells is one example.

It may not seem that the simple act of feeling discomfort in the body could dissolve stress. But while in the throes of exciting activity and strain, we usually don't notice the stress. The noticing is the shift of consciousness to a field where dissolution can begin. Faults exist within us because our inner security force hasn't yet caught them in its searchlights. When we first notice a fault we logically think that it has just then developed. Actually it may have gone through a long process of becoming conscious. Since its illusory nature can't stand the light, it starts to fade as soon as we see it. Furthermore, the bigger and blacker the problem seems, the quicker it will be gone. The saying, "It's always darkest before the dawn," is about the growth of a phenomenon to its final expression. The cry of the soul in anguish is the beginning of deliverance. It is said that Sri Ramakrishna, Swami Vivekananda's guru, so despaired of ever seeing his beloved goddess Kali that one day he seized a butcher knife with full intent to end a life he considered not worth living without her. She appeared instantly, and after that came every time he called.

Natural Law does not allow us, by control or artifice, to leapfrog over our negativity into the Promised Land. On the other hand, it requires no effort from us since what we are seeking is already our own. Therefore if cosmic effortlessness were to descend upon us right now we would suddenly find ourselves in the only true life. "Control is against life." This insight comes from Maharishi's knowledge of both meditation practice and daily living. It is what assured him at the beginning of his mission that if control was replaced by a technique that allowed the mind to follow its natural course to more and more happiness man would come out of suffering.

We said in Chapter Four that seeing and knowing spontaneously result in correction. This allows the mind to remain on its natural path without the deviations caused by effort and control. Control not only doesn't work, it stems from and reinforces dissatisfaction with the current state of our life, which is a drag on our sense of well-being. In addition, its unnaturalness constricts the mind and drives a wedge between seeing/knowing and the remedy that flows from deep levels.

We have discussed that by formulating solutions to problems on the gross level of thinking we may be diverting deep-level solutions into channels that are not right for us. Whereas, leaving the mind in a state of conscious unknowing—in reverence for the mysterious ways in which God works—puts the mind in a state of innocence that opens the doors to the Transcendent.

Effort and control disrupt the evolutionary force. They arise from the belief that our will is superior to Nature's will and lead in directions that may not be those of our true Self. ("Which of you by taking thought can add one cubit unto his stature?" Matt. 6:27.) And yet, we must do something if we are ever to come out of imperfection and problems. Simple seeing and knowing represent action upon ourselves that is at the same time free of effort. Natural, non-compulsive seeing and knowing keeps the force of evolution flowing upward from the source of Nature.

Effort may bring about changes, but it further constricts consciousness. We move from place to place in the same field. Only knowledge of what is outside the field can cause genuinely new and evolutionary things to happen. "Knowledge comes to him who is awake," Maharishi says. Everyone has experienced the immediate, powerful effect a single piece of knowledge can have on his life when he is ready for it, awake to it. Transcendental experience is pure wakefulness.

The act of looking within for solutions to problems is waking up to the growth occurring in the totality of the self and to begin to change the parts in the process of changing the whole. Self-referral brings our negativity into the total concept of who we are and is a way of asking for healing. The habit of object-referral, on the other hand, excludes those parts we don't want to see, and if this goes so far that we deny them as parts of the self, we exclude them from self-healing. We can eliminate only the self-delusions we can see. To look at reality is to dispel illusions. Instead of striving with our limited mental resourses, we awaken the unconscious to lead us to our true nature, which is transcendental consciousness, the ultimate self-observation.

The Self-referral Life

As a life-style, innocent non-compulsive Self-referral is the most graceful and efficient way to view the world because it allows all our daily tasks to be handled from a central computer that has access to all knowledge. The outer world is just the inner world of Self having taken forms according to a multitude of natural laws.

In fact, Natural Law is inseparable from the apparent materiality that structures our lives: The subatomic building blocks of matter not only arise from the quantum vacuum state obeying Law, they are made of Law. Physicists realized long ago that no single particle can be proved to be the smallest, only that it is not—by discovering a smaller one. Since this is an uncontestable truth, the only conclusion was that there is not a smallest particle and that in reality there is no particle at all. Manifest Nature raises itself up by its own bootstraps, by intentions of the Creator manifest as Natural Law. This is called the Bootstrap theory.

In his Vedic Science, Maharishi teaches that the vacuum of transcendental consciousness is the Home of Natural Law. All success in the world is based on knowing and obeying these laws. Every professional decision that we need for all achievement in life and every personal choice for inner health and happiness is known to the Self and accessed in increasing power and refinement by Self-referral. Instead of looking without and working for the fruits of the actions, we look within and follow where the joy of our work leads us. We don't have to deal with the multiplicity of things, only this one thing. The joy of our daily activity keeps us continually connected with Natural Law.

Fragmentation of thought (object referral) began with technology centuries ago—or, technology began with fragmentation of thought. In *Understanding Media* Marshall McLuhan recounts the story of a man, Tzu-Gung, traveling through China in the old days of the Empire. He sees an old man irrigating his vegetable patch one bucketful at a time from his well. "There is a way whereby you can irrigate a hundred ditches in one day," Tzu-Gung tells him, "and...with little effort." The gardener stood up and said, "And what would that be?" The traveler told him that you use a wooden lever, weighed at the back and light in front. In this way you can bring up water so quickly that it just gushes out. "This is called a draw well," he said. Then anger rose up in the old man's face, and he said, "I have heard my teacher say that whoever uses machines does all his work like a machine. He who does his work like a machine grows a heart like a machine, and he who carries the heart of a machine in his breast loses his simplicity. He who has lost his simplicity becomes unsure in the strivings of his soul. Uncertainty in the strivings of the soul is something which does not agree with honest sense. It is not that I do not know of such things; I am ashamed to use them."

Material technology is a result of the strivings of the relative mind and, if one isn't careful, produces only more strife. The last fifty years have proved that the more time-saving technology we have, the less time we have at our disposal. Our effectiveness is reduced and the quality of our work is compromised. Ninety percent of the best literature ever produced was written with a quill pen. Technology is a way to avoid working for the joy while focusing on the fruits.

We can imagine the man in his vegetable patch dividing his labor between his plants and the well. Alternation of activities provides rest. At the end of the day he is exercised in body, relaxed in mind and proud of his labor. He is not working for the fruits (or, in this case the vegetables) but for the joy of the actions. Thus all his attention is on the work, and the results are maximum. This is the wholeness of the self that we had use of in the agricultural age. It has been seriously compromised by technology. Technology is the first thing to tempt us when wholeness—Castaneda's "personal power"—is lost. Technology acts like a drug to awaken the drowsy; once we taste it, we must have more immediately. As individuals we rarely have the strength to go back. As a civilization, it is impossible.

Once our attention is turned to our inner health and happiness—which it does naturally when we understand the need to straighten up our field of consciousness—our personal power begins to be restored. We go deeper and deeper into Self, and thus find ourselves following the advice of the Vedas to "know the one thing by which all things known."

At the highest level of Self-referral living there is a sense of "being at home with everything," to use Maharishi's phrase—a feeling that everything is a part of you. This is fulfillment of St.

Paul's promise, "Having nothing, and yet possessing all things," (2Cor. 6:10): When transcendental consciousness replaces the finite mind, one has nothing because the Transcendent is uncreated. Yet, because that is the consciousness that created the universe, you own all things. Since everything comes from transcendental intelligence, your thoughts and feelings are awake at the creative level of everything you experience. You are in touch with every object, event, and situation at a level transcendental to external learning, where all is managed by Nature. This is real prosperity, which is often accompanied by a reduced need for material things. Having "the substance of things hoped for," makes one increasingly self-sufficient. In computing our real net worth, it is often better to make a list of what we can do without rather than a list of what we have.

We have lost so much of our personal power that "experts" have arisen in every area of life. Seminars are available to teach us how to take a walk. We can take a course on what to say on a date. Even in areas where others' advice is truly needful, Self-referral plays the more important part. It is obvious to people who are in the business of giving advice (like writers) that successful people who advise others didn't exactly get where they are by what they tell others to do. They did it by Self-referral (all true success is self-made) and then they present us with guidelines to follow by object-referral. Where their advice doesn't work (it usually doesn't) it's because it doesn't resonate with the hearer's inner knowledge. The rise of "the experts" is proof both of the complexity of modern life and the need for the simplicity of Self-referral. It is to this divide that modern life is leading us.

The proliferating technology that has made object-referral such a dominant force in our lives cannot be resisted or abandoned, but must be allowed to run its course. By its increasing sophistication, technology is able to accomplish more and more by doing less and less. How it can do this is illustrated by a graphic procedure in physics called inverse mapping: A line is drawn straight outward from the periphery of a circle, and in the opposite direction is continued inward toward the center. When the inward-moving line reaches the center, the other line has reached infinity. The procedure is meant to demonstrate that inner and outer are the same thing, and that "smaller than the smallest" (the dimensionless center) is identical to "larger than the largest" (infinity). Thus the Vedas refer to Brahm as the "dweller in the atom and the abode of all things." From this dimensionless (transcendental) center, infinite achievement is possible in a spontaneous manner. In this way, modern technology is proceeding on the principle of Nature's drive toward fulfillment, and man will not stop until he can accomplish everything by doing nothing. Sophisticated and confusing external technology will finally give way to a technology that is at the same time a state of Being—a technology of Pure Consciousness that is infinitely sophisticated and yet utterly simple.

Self-referral ultimately reunites us with Pure Consciousness and restores the wholeness, or holiness, of sanghitā. (*Whole*, from the Anglo-Saxon root *hal*, means holy or sound.) When we look at ourselves with only the intent to change, consciousness begins to dissolve the veil of concepts that has fragmented us, and starts to reestablish the togetherness of observer and observed. It was the primal act of Self-referral, when Rishi saw itself, that broke the One into the many; now applied to the many, it restores the One. For observer and observed to reunite, the process of observation must function with the primal innocence that originally characterized the togetherness of the three. Innocence, in this case, is both the mind's complete acceptance of the fundamental unity of observer, observed, and process of observation, and the heart's yearning for God.

Intuit Your Bad Self

We said earlier that Benedetto Croce equates intuition—framing our amorphous impressions into forms—with expression. This equation, he says, has to do with the "generally admitted truth [that] thought cannot exist without speech." That is, when the mind creates any thought or image, the process of expression begins on a subtle level which is technically speech.

In Croce's framing of amorphous feelings and impressions, they "pass by means of words...into the clarity of the contemplative spirit. It is impossible to distinguish intuition from expression in this cognitive process. One appears with the other at the same instant, because they are not two, but one."

Croce anticipated the entrance of subjectivity into the question of Reality that was brought out in quantum theory. (*Aesthetic* was published in 1901.) He says that unintuited impressions don't exist. Beyond intuition (perception) "are only impressions, sensations, impulses, feelings, and emotions that still fall short of the spirit and are not assimilated by man; something postulated for the convenience of exposition, while actually non-existent, since to exist is also a fact of the spirit." To be is to be perceived. Also an act of the spirit is the physicist's observation of the subatomic particle, which brings it from the formless vacuum state into relative existence.

It is the factor of expression that leads to Croce's point that "by elaborating his impressions [after having intuited them], man frees himself from them. By objectifying them, he removes them from him and makes himself their superior; for 'express' means 'to cast forth' as well as to articulate or artistically represent."

Thus, in the natural process by which we intuit our negative self, the myriad impressions are combined into a single concept that expresses them all—as a painting gives a single overall idea from its various, sometimes diverse, images. Let's say a spiritualist and writer seeking to avoid distractions goes to the West Indies and rent a small place. Before he knows what is happening, the romantic setting he has chosen begins to become a distraction itself. Everywhere he sees palm trees, white sand beaches, narrow cobblestone streets, quaint seventeenth-century Spanish buildings, and the colorful dress styles of the people. These creep into his consciousness with a new and exciting sense of life, to the point of influencing everything he does.

He is dealing with something very much like the negative self in the sense that he is facing a problem he has no choice but to live with. One day he has a realization in words of what he has been perceiving as amorphous impressions and sensations. He thinks, "Okay, I have a problem with the *romance*." On a deeper mental level than the impressions—that is, on the level of insight—a thought has occurred that wraps those impressions entirely. In a realization greater than the sum of the parts, he has framed them all and thus subordinated them. This is what Croce calls an act of the spirit because by speech he created the impressions. They had no real existence until he put them into a frame in which the gestalt is seen at a glance.

One has a sense of liberation as he gains superiority over the problem and drags it to a corner of the screen. And as a single mark better reveals the emptiness of a blank page, this one mark against him recreates the rest of himself as free. The expression of his problem has "cast it forth:" His view of himself is now that of the pure page, and the continued experience of life within this view will eliminate the problem completely, as a lawn planted with grass will eventually choke out the few patches of weeds.

This is not just on the level of the intellect; it yields an experience of the Transcendent, the spirit. A single mark on a blank page gives an experience of the unity of dynamism and silence as does hearing a far-off church bell in the quietness of the dawn. The poignant sense of wholeness that this arouses in us comes from sound and silence perceived simultaneously. This is the collapse of infinity (silence) to a point that is the first act of creation—the collapse of "Ah" to "Ka" (see Ch. 2). It is the integration of silence and dynamism that is Brahm. It gives an experience of the newness of creation, as does Croce's intuition, and restarts our life in purity.

William Blake said, "The road of excess leads to the palace of wisdom." Logically, this is as incomprehensible as the unity of silence and dynamism. But the sensory excess has only hidden the wholeness of consciousness, as the "romance" mentioned above clouded the writer's abilities. Thus, when the excess reaches critical mass it isolates itself into a separate category and the hidden self-knowledge appears immediately.

It may seem a curious irony that excess leads to wisdom but control does not. Control limits excess but also restricts expansion of the self. We must let our curiosity and imagination flow. Although these are the qualities to which St. Augustine attributed his heretical early life, if we give free rein to them and similar traits that enrich our humanity, the growing breadth of seeing and depth of knowing will allow us to separate the negative from the positive and, as Augustine did, rise above these "faults" into higher life.

Of course, Croce's intuition is not something we must *do* but something that occurs naturally. It is a genuine insight into the nature of consciousness. showing us that our ordinary perceptions are acts of the spirit.

The Eternal Moment

Because of the power of consciousness, Self-referral of the natural kind we have been discussing is a way to bring about change directly, without any intermediate agency. It helps one change who he is moment to moment, allowing him eventually to realize that in Reality he is the person who is observing himself from the peak of the "heavenly realm," at the top of Dante's hill.

Then who exactly is the person on the path? What is his reality as contrasted with his infinite Reality? In *The Spectrum of Consciousness* Ken Wilber says our reality is what we are experiencing now. "How many readers," Wilber asks, "would say that who they are is the consciousness that it reading this page right now?" But of course that is who we are; one's reality and what he is now experiencing are the same thing. The experiences of the past are dead, leaving only vestiges, and the future is unborn, only potential. The present is the only thing that is with us always. It is permanent. And permanence is the defining criterion of the Real—it is the only criterion.

But when we speak of the present moment, how long is the moment we have in mind? One second? The space between two thoughts? A camera can isolate 1/500th of a second. Then surely a moment is smaller than this. In reality it is dimensionless and eternal—the same way the dimensionless center of a circle is infinite.

In the end, whether the moment has dimension or is without dimension is determined by the capacity of the observer. Whether the Reality that is us at each moment is bound or boundless is determined by the observing consciousness. If that consciousness is infinite then the moment is exploded to infinity. ("To see infinity in a grain of sand and eternity in an hour," said Blake.) All is unbounded to unbounded awareness. To the observation of Pure Consciousness, we are not a creature of time but of eternity. Thus to our "heavenly" observer, we (the observed) are his identical twin.

We become so through repeated experience of transcendental consciousness as we climb the hill to Reality. In the experience, the observer and observed come increasingly close together through the ever-shortening process of observation.

The mind of the relative moment expands toward the infinity of Pure Consciousness unitl the observing process shrinks to nothing and the observed and observer disappear into each other. This experience was wonderfully captured in Donovan's song *Hurdy-Gurdy Man* (which he wrote immediately after his course with Maharishi in India) in which the first two lines represent the illusory action leading to transcending, and the last two present a picture of the Transcendent state in which we have always lived:

> Thrown like a star by the sea
> I opened my eyes to take a peek
> To find that I was by the sea
> Gazing with tranquility.

Chapter 9

The World as Myself

The author William Gibson coined the term "cyberspace" to denote the ambiguous area behind a computer screen where data reside and where other forms of space are created for playing games. Racecars, baseball players, and ninja warriors appear solid and so we perceive space between them. But actually the space the objects and the depth owe themselves solely to different colored dots, which are nothing but tiny balls of electric energy that contain information. It's the same thing when we look into world-space, as Benton showed with his "supermicroscope" (Ch. 2, "What Hath Rishi Wrought?"): The objects and the spaces are made of the same stuff, differing only in arrangement and quantify. This "stuff" is my consciousness. The outer world and my responses to it are the same thing. Maharishi says, "The world is as you are."

An Experiment in Subjective Science

When Rishi (the seer) observes Chhandas (the object) he sees another part of himself in the unity of sanghitā. This is the basic experience in *Maharishi Nadi Vigyan*—Maharishi's revival of the subjective science of self-pulse diagnosis found in ancient Ayur-Veda. By this self-diagnosis, this act of Self-referral, the mind sees the physiology on a very refined level and thus the two are brought closer together.

Ancient Ayur-Veda identified three pulses on the radial artery in the wrists. They issue ultimately from Rishi, Devata and Chhandas. When this unified Absolute level of existence manifests as the subtlest relative level, the three are called the gunas—sattwa, rajas, tamas—creation, maintenance and dissolution. The pulses issue in turn from the three gunas and are called *vata, pitta, and kapha.* Their behavior indicates the state of balance or imbalance (unity or disunity) in the physiology.

The reading of the pulses tells the individual which Maharishi Ayur-Vedic herbal preparations to use to rectify any imbalances. These herbal decoctions have been restored to their original purity by Maharishi with the help of Indian Ayur-Vedic physicians who are sensitive to the corruption of their formulas over time. The decoctions restore balance in the physiology through sound: The vibratory rates of the plants used and the synergistic frequencies of different plants combined, straighten out discordant frequencies in the nervous system that cause imbalance and disease.

But the self-referral practice of Maharishi Nadi-Vigyan brings a benefit of different sort. Because mind and body are two locations on the same continuum of manifestation, the condition of the physiology is the condition of consciousness. Thus if my awareness is foggy I will not get a clear reading of my pulse, which of itself will be in a muddled state. If my mind is clear I will get a clear reading of the pulse, which correspondingly will be in a stable state. Therefore in Maharishi Nadi-Vigyan one has a direct experience that consciousness and the physiology function as the same thing. This may be the closest experiential verification we have of quantum theory's finding (and Maharishi's assertion) that the world is as one's consciousness is. That is, because when my consciousness is unclear, I will experience the world at large, starting with my body, as disordered and confused, which is the actual state of the world as far as this one individual is concerned. It will be different for another person and different for me in another state of consciousness.

We can confirm this principle by reflecting on those days when we were dull and disenergized and everything went wrong. On days when we are rested, fresh and full of hope everything turns out in our favor. The world is not the objective phenomenon it has been thought to be. It is a potentiality that manifests (that is, becomes dynamic) in the manner in which it is observed.

We said above that the self-referral act of pulse diagnosis brings consciousness closer to the unity of sanghitā. When the fingers touch the pulses and the attention goes to them, there is an immediate settling of the activity of the mind, so that the swirl of consciousness becomes more integrated. The mind-body balance that the practice helps bring about is the unity of Rishi, Devata, and Chanddas.

Fully developed individuals—those whose mental functioning has risen to the permanently stable state beyond duality—say that the world is an ever-changing dream spun out of our consciousness like a spider's web. As in a nocturnal dream, we made the concepts and hold the beliefs and expectations that created it. This intellectual understanding opens the door to ultimately experiencing it as self caused. But even in the short run it is important to a clear understanding of where our problems and obstacles come from. Without understanding the world as the self, we will forever regard our problems as externally caused and tend to think that life is unfair. In the frustration and grief that this brings, we will never see that the situation can be changed by changing ourselves. We abandon our birthright as Creator of our own destiny.

The World as a Viewpoint

In his relativity theories Einstein in effect showed that the world is a point of view. One of his famous thought experiments went like this: A man stands at a railroad track and hears a train approaching. Coming toward him its sound builds up into a high-pitched "eeee!" sound. When it passes it changes to a drawn-out "oouu" sound. These relative sounds make us ask, "What sound is the train *really* making? Einstein proved that it doesn't make a real sound; that is, a sound independent of the observer's position.

The sound the train is really making is the sound of one hand clapping. In the instant the train is directly in front of the man it changes from one sound to the other; and in that change there is a dimensionless moment in which duality and manifestation subside. (Maharishi has said that whenever one thing changes into another—even the change from one thought to another—there is something in between that is neither.) Thus there is no objective sound. We create the sound by our point of view, our consciousness. Of course this doesn't mean that in the ideal state of life one hears no sounds, although Enlightened teachers speak of a "silent world," and Maharishi says that, with each higher level of consciousness there is a more profound silence. Of course Maharishi hears the relative sounds of the train, but simultaneously the Absolute sound of silence.

The world has been likened to a gigantic fisherman's net with a glass bead at every intersection of its cords. Each bead holds a reflection of all the other beads but from a slightly different perspective. Like this, you and I see the same tree from a slightly different point of view. But in reality are we looking at exactly the same tree? Each of us turns the tree's vibrational frequencies (transcendental sounds) into matter in terms of himself, and *that* is the only tree that can be seen. The other one is a quantum tree waiting to be created by someone else.

Those who hold this Vedic view of the world have been asked whether the tree exists if no one sees it. Yes and no. We have mentioned the dictum of George (Bishop) Berkeley that to be is to be perceived. A man named Ronald Knox challenged this with a limerick:

There was a young man who said, God
Must think it exceedingly odd
    If he finds that this tree
    Continues to be
When there's no one about in the Quad.

Berkeley replied:

Dear Sir:
    Your astonishment's odd:
I am always about in the Quad.
    And that's why the tree
    Will continue to be,
Since observed by
    Yours faithfully,
        God.

The Garden of Forked Paths

The nature of our response to the world is the nature of the world. To *notice* is the key to applying quantum theory to individual consciousness. If we don't notice when something strikes our consciousness, we don't create it. (We don't "intuit" it, to use Croce's term.) This is governed by what Aldous Huxley called the "reducing valve." According to who we are by our past experiences, our consciousness spontaneously filters out certain things that other people will see, hear, etc. However, when we notice, we bring the experience forth from the quantum field; we "pop the quiff" in the phrase of physicist Fred Alan Wolf: Noticing frees the potential object of experience (or in the case of the physicists, the electron) from the quantum wave function ("quiff" for short), which is an undulating probability that the experience/electron will occur. But it always occurs when we notice and never when we don't. An electron is such a thing—actually a non-thing—that physicists say it is impossible to know what it is doing when they're not around. If we could know how an electron behaves when we are not looking at it, we could know what an experience is that we didn't have.

Stress in the physiology darkens consciousness and acts as the reducing valve. Acquiring stress is an ongoing feature of human life. So is the neutralization of it. Because of the intimate relationship of body and mind, stress release is often accompanied by some degree of turbulence in consciousness, as we discussed earlier. To accommodate this turbulence the mind experiences random thoughts. The neutraliztion of stress is both a long-term friend and an short-run enemy: It is impossible to think of a world without this natural, liberating process; but in the process of freeing consciousness, it can temporarily cloud perception.

When our vibratory rate is upset by stress and its neutralization, it may undergo a change analogous to a low-pressure area that allows stormy weather to rush in. But since this happens to most of us regularly, the cause is difficult to identify—and moreso if we immediately emotionalize the negativity, which we usually do.

The senses that perceive loud disturbing music coming from the next apartment, for example, provide no clue to this truth. Reason is overcome by the emotions the music is causing. As in the case of a rainbow, which exists in the mind, everything in these sounds, including the gestalt, appear to be precisely locatable in the causal vibrations, but actuality nothing whatsoever in what I am hearing can be separated from the condition of my consciousness. It would have been easier for medieval man to divine that the earth goes around the sun than for us to guess that the universe which seems so implacably objective is in reality nothing but the self made visible. Actually what I am doing is using the loud music to create a karmically necessary disturbance for myself.

Let's say that because of this I get to bed late, get up late, and eat breakfast late. Not being hungry at lunch I go for a walk, and in so doing I realize that this is what I needed. I find the change of habit refreshing. Ideas come to me and in the end something productive and enlivening happens that proves I needed the change.

As I walk along by the lagoon I recall that some physicists say our responses send out new universes of thought and behavior in different directions moment to moment, and that ultimately all these roads lead to Rome. So, even wrong is right. I recall the scripture that everything turns out for good for those who love the Lord.

Alternately, if I had known the real cause of my being disturbed, I would have seen that it was the reality of the moment, the only possible reality. I would have remembered that what happens is the only thing that can happen. I would have understood the "disturbance" as actually caused by my mental turbulence brought about by the physiological purification of stress release. In this scenerio nothing happens. I sleep. I re-destine what was destined by my potential karma and start with a fresh universe. I wouldn't have needed the walk because I had already learned what it taught me. For those who seek the Transcendent, even wrong is right; but right is righter.

The Only Game in Town

The spectacle of yogamaya discussed in Ch. 2, ("Ved and Veda-lila) as the veil that hides Reality is much more delightful than we have made it by believing it real. Learning how to play the game at its most enjoyable is how we pierce through to the Uncreated. The consciousness that struggles against a deceiver we made up—and who therefore knows how to prick and probe our every weakness—must become one of blissful, careless play. We must become as a little child. This style of consciousness develops by watching ourselves struggle until we see that all is vanity.

It has been said that we play games because God first plays a game. The only real difference between athletics, for example, and other businesses or professions is that the game is not about a product or a service. There is the money, of course, but the game is primarily about the game itself. Even though professional football is big business, men play it because they love the game. Truly successful business people and entrepreneurs are made because they love to play the game. What distinguishes a game from work is that the deposits of joy in the soul are more important than the deposits of money in the bank. That deposits in the "storehouse of impressions" (Ch. 5—Action, Impression, Desire) are the only things we can take with us confirms that the ultimate purpose is the joy of the actions, not the fruits.

But the cosmic game of maya (or whatever we choose to call the great illusion) has not been taught to us as a game. It is a mystery we have to unravel on our own. Maya reveals itself as a game only by our realizing the Reality behind it. Failing this, we create "real" outcomes from the unreal. But the world we see is no more real than a movie. Our expectations of real material outcomes is as absurd as an actor expecting to spend stage money he received in a movie scene.

When we know intellectually and by direct experience that this is not a solid world of material outcomes, we are established in the Real outcome, the great Uncreated. Krishna, who spins yogamaya out of himself for our delight, provides definitive instructions for playing the game in Ch. 2, v. 48 of the *Bhagavad-Gita*: "Established in Yoga (unity with Being), perform action." This is the cosmic consciousness we will discuss in the next chapter. Under this condition not only has our vision risen above illusion, but thus freed, infinite intelligence is brought to bear upon the actions. The laws of Nature, which are *our* laws, written by us before the world was, spontaneously support the success of every action, and our cup runs over.

At the end of *Steppenwolf* Harry Haller has a vision of Mozart in the Magic Theatre. Mozart represents a spiritual artist who has cut through the illusion and *sees*. He switches on a small cheap radio on which a Handel concerto is playing. He tells Haller that he must hear the truth behind the tinny sound that distorts and falsifies it—and that to do this he must free his own mind of distortions. We have to see what's the matter with ourselves before we can see what's the "matter" with the world.

I Am the Cause

We are the cause throughout our life of everything that happens to us good and bad. We cause the world by how we see it; we create it in our own image. When we free ourselves of distortions, we are no longer *of* the world we are in. We are transcendental, ultimate cause. We have died to matter and resurrected the eternal spirit.

On this basis Paul could say, "O death where is thy sting? O grave where is thy victory?" He wrote these words in what some spiritualists call the "heaven-world," where the great transition is known for the illusion that it is. In the words of the St. Frances prayer, "dying," by which "we are born into eternal life," doesn't wait for the death of the body. Nor does bodily death by itself bring eternal life regardless of what we may have been led to believe.

"I am the cause" is the great divide. One who can truthfully utter these words has separated a past, in which he was buffeted about by every ill wind, from a future where goodness and mercy will follow him all the days of his life. One who understands and experiences himself as the sole cause of his conditions will learn how to live; one who doesn't, won't.

Chapter 10

Maharishi's Meditation Programs
And Higher States of Consciousness

"The final measure of a man is his vision." This book has been a vision of the Absolute—the field of all possibilitiies—and I hope it makes clear that, as Maharishi says, "nothing is impossible for man on earth." Intellectual understanding of Maharishi's programs gives a vision of these possibilities; regular direct experience makes them realities.

At the end of Chapter Eight we talked about the eternal moment when the field of thought is transcended. The mind will come out of this state only when it is forced to. The awareness will remain transcendental, even in the midst of dynamic thought and action, unless acted upon by an external force.

This force is stress in the physiology. In transcendental silence much stress is neutralized. The release of stress, being physical, causes subtle movements in the body that, owing to the intimate mind/body connection, are accompanied by movements in the mind. This movement is thought. Early in one's experience as a meditator, the mind will come out of the Transcendent to have a thought. Thoughts may be about something we have had on our mind during the day, or in some cases they are a recalling of the event that produced the stress long before. The thoughts are quite ordinary.

Between this beginning stage and the state of cosmic consciousness (spontaneous maintenance of Being during all thought and action) there is an intermediate level that indicates growth toward that Enlightenment. In this level the mind begins to experience subtle thoughts while awareness remains transcendental. This is a foretaste of the permanent maintenance of transcendental consciousness with thought and action. The physiology noticeably functions at a very refined level, and the subtle thoughts that come are accompanied by feelings of expansion and bliss.

When this begins to happen regularly the body is becoming considerably less stressed, and consciousness is beginning to function on a significantly higher level in daily life. The deep knowing previously buried in the unconscious is becoming available for conscious use.

"Life is different in different levels of consciousness," Maharishi says. One of his contributions to modern spirituality is the division of peoples' levels of consciousness into distinct categories. Each level has its own style of physiological functioning, and consciousness is based on the way the physiology functions. Therefore different instructions are needed at each level. A large part of the confusion in modern spirituality is because people are expected to follow teachings that are either beyond them are behind them.

Maharish calls the first level "ignorance" (*avidya*, or nonknowledge). The second level is reached when the mind begins to experience transcendental consciousness. The third level stretches from the onset of transcendental experience to the establishment of cosmic consciousness. Cosmic consciousness is gained through regular transcendental experience alternated with unstrained activity during the day. Beyond that are the higher states of God consciousness and unity consciousness.

Cosmic consciousness is full awareness of the Self including what was previously unconscious. Although this means the end of the cycle of birth and death, it cannot be the highest state because it is one of duality. But this is not the type of duality we have been discussing up to now. It is not the duality experienced in relaltivity. It is a "perfect duality," Maharishi says, "between total awareness of the Self and limited awareness of the relative world." It is duality between inner and the outer. Inner and outer are the same thing ultimately, as we have discussed, but in cosmic consciousness the individual is aware of a profound separation. Perception, although much more subtle than before, must rise to experience the "other" (the relative world) as the Self. This happens through daily living, Maharishi says, and through love. He says that devotion to God can never be complete until cosmic consciousness, because until then we have no fully realized Self to offer.

Cosmic consciousness is natural maintaince of the pure wakefulness of Being along with the three relative states of consciousness, waking, dreaming and (even) sleeping. In waking state, all our thought and action is spontaneously in accord with the totality of Nature Law. Technically there would be no dreaming because the stress release which causes that illusory consciousness would no longer be necessary. In sleep we are the silent witness of that most profound rest, which Maharishi calls "sweet, deep sleep."

Types of Meditation

There are three major types of spiritual practices that are generally lumped under the term "meditation." One is concentration. This is what we do at work when we have to focus the mind on a fixed point of attention. It's the last thing we want to do in our morning and evening meditation. Maharishi regards spiritual practices that hold the mind to a fixed point as a injurious to life. Forced focus, such as concentration on a desired goal—even a goal like "God" or "Love"—tires the mind and weakens it for necessary concentration in daily life. What the mind does in meditation must be opposite and complementary to its ordinary waking-state activity; that is, it must be the silence that is the complementary opposite of dynamism.

Contemplation is another type of mental focus but is less rigid. Here the practitioner chooses a concept that he wants to inculcate, say a verse of scripture, and quietly examines it from various angles of thought. In this process he may gain insights that are of value to him. But whatever he gains will be only a small part of the whole: If he learns to love his neighbor as himself, he will later have to choose another topic of contemplation to help him overcome the frustration of sitting in a traffic jam.

If concentration techniques hold the mind to one point on the surface of the ocean, and contemplation allows some swimming around, real meditation takes the mind to the ocean floor, where Gilgamesh found the Plant of Immortality. The defining characteristic of meditation is *the systematic reduction of the activity of thought itself—a settling of the electrical impulses in the brain*—until it arrives at the thoughtless state, which is infinity. This is unbounded awareness. The mind achieves full wakefulness in eternal silence. Like an audiotape that plays on after the music has stopped, experience is there but there is no object of experience. This technique, far from being tedious and tiring, is the most enjoyable and refreshing "activity" the mind can undertake.

Maharishi refers to concentration and contemplation techniques in his commentary to *Gita* Ch. 2, v. 55.

> Such practices, remaining as they do on the level of thinking, can at best create moods of the mind; they certainly do not produce the state of mind called 'steady intellect'. This results only from direct experience of pure consciousness to such a degree of clarity that the difference between the 'ultimate' and the 'non-ultimate' is clearly cognized and appreciated on the intellectual level as well....

Shankara clearly says that this state of steady intellect is produced by the practice of transcending relativity as expressed in [Ch. 2] verse 45 and not by merely spinning words about it or merely trying to understand it....

Maharishi goes on to discuss the two primary paths of the spiritual life.

This should be sufficient to remove the misunderstanding created by commentators or translators of the *Bhagavad-Gita* who hold that the steady intellect can only be gained by recluses, a view that is responsible for spiritual decadence in modern society. Unfortunately, Shankara's own view has been misrepresented by commentators who undertook to propagate his philosophy. They seem to have missed the central part of spiritual life—transcendental consciousness as the direct way to its realization. As a result, everything that aimed at clarifying the process of transcending has been held to belong to the path of renunciation and attributed to the recluse way of life. This lack of insight into principle cast the center of spiritual life onto the recluse order, thus debarring the householder from the gains of spirituality and throwing the whole of humanity out of joint.

This verse [Ch. 2, v. 55] does not record any outer sign of a man whose intellect is steady and who is established within the Self, because there cannot be any outer sign to show that a man is absorbed deep within himself. The inner state of such a man cannot be judged by outer signs. It cannot be said that he sits like this or like that or closes his eyes in any particular manner. No such external signs can serve as criteria of this state.

A man may sit in any style and go deep within himself and be in bliss consciousness.

The mind always seeks a field of greater charm. In the realm of spiritual practice, concentration is inherently difficult. The mind seeks its own still waters until it leaves thinking behind altogether and is *held concentrated naturally*, without doing, by its own thirst for bliss. Not by concentration is the mind held concentrated effortlessly. This is the Self-referral we have discussed, but here it is brought to its highest level and has infinite power to heal. It is return to the primal state of sanghitā in which the knower (the meditator), the process of knowing (the meditation) and the known (the goal of meditation) are one.

We have said that the mind will leave this state only because the rest it achieves causes a release of stress in the physiology that produces mental activity. Thus when the mind fails to reach the Transcendent in a meditation sitting it is because the rest it achieves on the way causes stress release which keeps the mind in activity. When this stress then gone, it is more likely that the mind will transcend next time. When the physiology is stress free, the mind will rest in the Transcendent "like a candle in a windless place," as the Vedas say. ("Be still and know that I am God," Ps. 46:10). This has been the experience of many throughout the ages—mystics, poets, scientists, artists, prophets and ordinary people—because it is the mind's natural state. In *Lines Written a Few Miles above Tintern Abby*, Wordsworth spoke of

> That serene and blessed mood
> In which the affections gently lead us on
> Until the breath of this corporeal frame,
> And even the motion of our human blood
> almost suspended,
> We are lain asleep in body and become a
> living soul,
> While with an eye made quiet by the power
> of harmony
> And the deep power of joy
> We see into the life of things.

Transcending also fulfills an instruction of Krishna in the *Bhagavad-Gita* that is central to Maharishi's teaching. It's the corollary to the verse discussed earlier (Ch. 2, v. 48) dealing with performing action in the state of Being. Ch. 2, v. 45 says:

"The Vedas concern is with the three gunas; be without the three gunas, O Arjuna." We have seen that the gunas are the three fundamental forces of creation, maintanence, and dissolution residing at the quantum level of phenomenality. They are thought of in two ways. Spiritualists may regard them as embodiments: Brahmá, Vishnu and Shiva respectively. Maharishi thinks of them as principles, Natural Laws, the permutations and combinations of which give rise to and govern the universe. They are the subtlest field of Nature we leave behind in transcending. Beyond that there is only the creative silence of the Uncreated. By saying, "Be without the three gunas," Krishna is urging Arjuna to go beyond the subtlest field of creation, to transcend the field, and thus gain the unity of thought and Being that world spirituality has sought for thousands of years by cultivating the *thought* of Being, or the *thought* of God.

Maharishi's insight that Krishna is actually talking about transcending the phenenomenal world contrasts sharply with modern Indian interpretations of this verse and is an example of Maharishi's insight. One such interpretation says that since, in Ayur-Veda, foods are classified according to the three gunas (and in this case called vata, pitta, or kapha) one must go on a fast in order to be without the three gunas. Another says that, since people also are classified by their mind/body types as vata, pitta, and kapha, one should isolate himself from others as a recluse in order to transcend the gunas.

Maharishi Transcendental Meditation

St. John of the Cross spoke of the senses as the enemies that inhabit a man's house (Ch. 4, "The Negative Self"). The senses cannot be controlled by will power and effort; that is, on their own level. In Ch. 3, v 7 of the *Gita* Krishna says, "He, who controlling the senses by the mind, without attachment…he excels, O Arjuna." The senses must be controlled by the mind because mind is basic to the senses. Maharishi comments:

> This is the simple technique by which the senses of perception are automatically controlled and organized...nothing need be done save to infuse the mind with transcendental consciousness...[in this state] the senses remain on their objects and the mind remains established in Being.

In experiencing the Transcendent, the mind becomes the transcendental Creator, Brahm: When experience is not of an object, the mind *becomes* what is experienced. Thus the *Upanishads* say, "To know Brahm is to be Brahm." All the positive attributes the mind might cultivate one at a time belong to it by transcending thought. Only through Absolute experience can one really come to love his neighbor as himself, for example, since only there are the two essentially the same thing. Nor can concentration or contemplation fulfill the first of Christ's two commandments: "Thou shalt love the Lord thy God with all thy heart, with all thy soul, and with all thy mind," (Matt. 22:37): The heart, soul, and mind achieve their full expressions only by functioning from the level of the Transcendent.

Most people think meditation is something you have to *do*. But significant reduction of the electrical impulses in the brain obviously cannot be accomplished by doing. As we have discussed, Maharishi Transcendental Meditation acts as a trigger that allows mental activity to settle of its own accord. After this first step the meditation goes almost by itself. It is a deceptively simple procedure.

There is no philosophy, religion or lifestyle connected with the practice. Transcendental Meditation operates only on the two principles of increasing charm and the reduction of sound, which in this case are related. The mind moves inward because enjoyment is greater at each subtler level of thought. The trigger that allows this to happen is the mantra and the technique for using it. The mantra is a special word that, being free of any meaning, doesn't get the intellect involved. Maharishi describes mantra as "a sound whose effects are known." Everyone knows the effects of a beautiful piece of music—sounds to soothe the savage beast—in comparison to the siren blasts of an emergency vehicle. The mantra is not spoken but entertained only in thought and thus is experienced as a mental sound. It is individualized for each person in order to produce maximum resonance with the vibratory rate of the individual's nervous system. Because there is no attempt to concentrate or hold on to the mantra, extraneous thoughts come and go; but always on a deeper level as the mantra is experienced in subtler states (the reduction of sound). The mantra is only the vehicle of meditation; that is, we don't meditate on the mantra, as people are wont to say. What we meditate on are increasingly refined levels of the thinking process. The following is from an appendix to Maharishi's commentary on the *Bhagavad-Gita*.

When a wave of the ocean makes contact with deeper levels of water, it becomes more powerful. Likewise, when the conscious mind expands to embrace deeper levels of thinking, the thought-wave becomes more powerful.

The expanded capacity of the conscious mind increases the power of the mind and results in added energy and intelligence. Man, who generally uses only a small portion of the total mind that he possesses, begins to make use of his full mental potential.

The technique may be defined as turning the attention inwards towards the subtler levels of a thought until the mind transcends the experience of the subtlest level of the thought and arrives at the source of thought. This expands the conscious mind and at the same time brings it in contact with the creative intelligence that gives rise to every thought.

A thought-impulse starts from the silent creative center within, as a bubble starts from the bottom of the sea. As it rises, it becomes larger; arriving at the conscious level of the mind, it becomes large enough to be appreciated as a thought, and from there it develops into speech and action.

Turning the attention inwards takes the mind from the experience of a thought at the conscious level to finer states of the thought until the mind arrives at the source of thought. This inward march of the mind results in the expansion of the conscious mind.

The technique is described as Transcendental Meditation.

Its practice is simple. There are no prerequisites for beginning the practice, other than receiving instructions personally from a qualified teacher.

It should be noted that Transcendental Meditation is neither a matter of contemplation nor of concentration. The process of contemplation and concentration both hold the mind on the conscious thinking level, whereasTranscendental Meditation systematically takes the mind to the source of thought, the pure field of creative intelligence.

We have spoken of the source of thought as the Transcendent, transcendental consciousness, Pure Consciousness, Atma, pure wakefulness, and the Absolute. These terms give understanding but don't describe the experience. We said above that one can experience transcendental consciousness along with faint, ordinary thoughts. But in the very earliest stages, one may transcend and experience nothing. This is a condition of being blinded by the light because nervous system is not yet cultured enough for such effulgence. In this case, in returning to thought one may have the sense that he has briefly been someplace that he can't identify..

We have also spoken of the source of thought as the Self. In more advanced stages, this experience is the "clearest of the clear," to use Tennyson's words quoted earlier. But it is difficult to describe because we have nothing to refer it to. It is bliss, and in its full expression is beyond the ecstacy we may have experienced externally from any object, event, or idea. It is the bliss of sudden release from the prison we thought was life. It is the bliss of the infinite and the eternal, the bliss of the highest God, *and yet it is experienced as Myself.*

Transcendental Meditation is designed to do just one thing: let the mind take its own course. This is anathema to those who believe the mind is inherently evil and needs to be controlled. But all the evil that preys upon man is a result of the control of life that has kept him from his true nature.

The impulse to control thoughts arises from ignorance of the mind's natural tendency to evolve from human to Divine. We have seen that this is counter-intuitive, but all the evil that preys upon man is a result of the control of life that has kept him from his true nature.

The ignorance and bondage that grow from stress and warp our perceptions are not free-floating errors. They are the distortions of something Real. The three beasts that have sent us on our journey around the cosmos are merely misapprensions of something good, infantile strivings for the Divine. To achieve our goals, freedom is essential. By holding on to lower-case good we remain in the field from which our errors arise.

By controlling the mind we struggle against evolution rather than flow with it. The best we can hope for from this outmoded spiritual philosophy is to someday happen upon the Transcendent by accident.

Searching for Shankara

Maharishi has reduced the whole of the spiritual quest to one easy-to-practice technique which, because it allows the mind to access the source of creation, lifts all the individual aspects of life holistically, in one stroke. This should not be surprising. We have discussed the loss and revival of the Supreme Knowledge over millennium-long cycles. At the low points of these cycles man forgets that he is born in bliss, sustained in bliss and goes again to bliss. He forgets that God's gift of bliss consciousness naturally requires man's knowledge of how to access it. Thousands of years of darkness have taught us that struggle, suffering and waiting for the afterlife are our only recourse. When we understand, with William Blake, that by cleaning the doors of perception "man will see life as it really is, infinite," the whole of the spiritual quest is reduced to the one objective of tuning the instrument of perception. Maharishi and Guru Dev identified the problem as wear and tear on the nervous system—passed on from generation to generation through past karma and genes—and devised a technique to provide the mind and body with the maximum degree of stress-neutralizing rest.

What follows is Dr. Franklin Merrell-Wolfe's story of his personal search to be without the three gunas, to locate transcendental consciousness. This is from the second chapter of his book, *The Philosophy of Consciousness without an Object*.

It was during the period when I was a student in the Graduate School of Philosophy of Harvard University in 1912-13 that, finally, I became convinced of the probable existence of a mode of consciousness that could not be comprehended within the limits of our ordinary forms of knowledge....

Ultimately, I found one oriental Sage with whose thought and temperment I felt a high degree of sympathetic rapport. This Sage was the Vedantic philosopher known as Shankara. I found myself in striking agreement with the more fundamental phases of his thought and was quite willing to apply the highly intellectual technique that he had charted. It was in this Sage's writings that I finally found the means that were effective in producing the transformation I sought....

Early in my studies I found that the manuals emphasized the necessity of killing out desire. This proved to be a difficult step to understand and far from easy to accomplish. Desire and sentient life are inseparable, and so it seemed as though this demand implied the equivalent of self-extinction. It was only after some time that I discovered that the real meaning consisted in a changing of the polarization of desire. Ordinarily, desire moves toward objects and objective achievements, in some sense. It is necessary that this desire should be given another polarization so that, instead of objects and achievements in the world field being sought, an eternal and all-encompassing consciousness should be desired....

Here Dr. Merrell-Wolfe's education and training seem to have led him to intuit what the final goal must be.

Here Dr. Merrell-Wolfe's education and training seem to have led him to intuit what the final goal must be.

Though there remained vast quantities of objective secular information of which I was ignorant and that I could have acquired, and there were many experiences that I had never sampled, yet I realized that, as such, they were void of depth and had no more value than David Hume's game of backgammon....
There was a critical point at which the shifting polarization had attained something like a neutral balance. At this point there was no decisive wish to go either way and the whole field of interest took on a colorless quality....I found it necessary to supplement the neutral state of desire by a forcibly willed resolution, and thus proceed in the chosen direction regardless of the absence of inclination. However, once past the critical point, the inward polarization of desire developed rapidly, and presently spontaneous inclination rendered the forcibly willed resolution unnecessary.

In addition to the barrier of desire directed toward external objects, the manuals specify a very important and closely related barrier to attainment. This is egoism. The strong feeling for, and attachment to, egoistic differentiation is an insurmountable barrier to a kind of consciousness that, instead of being discrete, and ego bound, is continuous, free, and impersonal. So a certain critical degree of dissolution or solution of egoistic crystallization must be effected if the transformation of consciousness is to be successful. I did not find it difficult to appreciate the logic of this requirement, but again, as in the case of outwardly polarized desire, the difficult part was the actual dissolution of the egoistic feeling. (The strong attachment for egoistic differentiation—that is, for duality—is an addiction we have acquired. It is the Mother of All Addictions, requiring nothing short of spiritual Self-illumination to overcome it.) The ordinary technique is the practice of practical altruism until personal self-consideration sinks well into the background. But this is not the only means that effects this result.

Merrell-Wolfe's conviction that Self-illumination is necessary to overcome the addiction of duality would find perfect agreement with Maharishi.

A desire for the transcendent Self and a love of universals also tend toward the quiet melting of the egoistic feeling. In this part of the discipline I found that my already established love of mathematics and philosophy was an aid of radical importance that, supplemented by more tangible practices, finally produced the requisite degree of melting.

During the last few weeks just preceding the transformation, there grew within me a strong expectation and a kind of inner excitement. I felt within me an indefinable assurance that, at last, the culminating success of a long search was within reach....

Finally, on the seventh of August, 1936, after having completed the reading of Shankara's discussion of "Liberation," as given in the *System of Vedanta* by Paul Deussen, I entered upon a course of meditative reflection upon the material just read. While engaged in this reflection, it suddenly dawned upon me that a common error in meditation—and one which I had been making right along---lay in the seeking of a subtle object or experience. Now, an object or an experience, no matter how subtle, remains other than the supersensible substantially. Thus the consciousness to be sought is the state of pure subjectivity without an object. This consideration rendered clear to me the emphasis, repeatedly stated by the manuals, upon the closing out of the modifications of the mind. But I had never found it possible to completely silence thought. *So it occurred to me that success might be attained simply by a discriminative isolation of the subjective pole of consciousness, with the focus of consciousness placed upon this aspect, but otherwise leaving the mental processes free to continue in their spontaneous functioning--they, however, remaining on the periphery of the attentive consciousness* [emphasis added]."

After arriving at the crucial understanding that the goal is not an object but consciousness without an object, Merrell-Wolfe was able to actualize it by allowing thoughts to come and go while attention remained on subjectivity. This involved accepting the contradiction that thought can be silenced by letting it continue.

Even a practitioner of Transcendental Meditation may not realize how heroic this is, so simple are Maharishi's instructions for accomplishing it.

> [Then] I saw that genuine Recognition is simply a realization of Nothing, but a Nothing that is absolutely substantial and identical with the SELF. This was the final turn of the Key that opened the Door. I found myself at once identical with the Voidness, Darkness, and Silence, but realized them as utter, though ineffable, Fullness, in the sense of Substantiality, Light, in the sense of Illumination...in the sense of pure formless Meaning and Value. The deepening of consciousness that followed at once is simply inconceivable and quite beyond the possibility of adequate representation. To suggest the Value of this transcendental state of consciousness requires concepts of the most intensive possible connotation and the modes of expression that indicate the most superlative value art can devise. Yet the result of the best effort seems a sorry thing when compared with the immediate Actuality. All language, as such, is defeated when used as an instrument of protrayal of the transcendent.

This last point about the the insufficiency of language is one of the many correspondences between Merrell-Wolfe's search and the process of Transcendental Meditation: The Taittiriya Upanishad says: "From where speech rebounds, that is My abode.")

We mentioned Maharishi's teaching that transcending the phenomenal universe is the only truly essential activity for complete success in the spiritual quest and in life in general.

He has reduced the technique for achieving this to essentials so that anyone can have it through regular practice and avoid the Herculean labors Merrell-Wolfe had to work through for nearly a quarter of a century.

Effortless Doing

In Plato's metaphor of the two horses (Ch. 4, "Consciousness of the Unconscious") we saw that the final unity of passion and reason occurs when reason renounces its age-old struggle against passion and begans to assimilate its energizing force. At the ordinary thinking level of the mind, reason can never make friends with passion's destructive frenzy, much less draw from it. This can occur only in the Transcendent where the whole brain is silent and the two opposite forces are indistinguishable. Through the regular experience of transcending thought, this unity rises into the thinking mind and we begin to give up the fruitless struggle against our evil twin, whom we now know is an indispensible part of ourself. The two sides of our nature begin to develop together, free to run in perfect unity in the field of their dreams where passion is reasonable and reason passionate.

This is balanced functioning of the left and right hemispheres of the brain; it is maintained in daily life as transcendental consciousness comes to cohere with thought and action (cosmic consciousness). Reason's rightful realm is the conscious thinking level of the mind, while passion, intuition, and holistic thinking are deeper functions and sometimes unconscious. When the mind becomes fully conscious in the state of cosmic consciousness, we are clearly aware of the deep intuitions that formerly guided our lives unconsciously. As we saw earlier, only when these impulses are unconscious are they threatening.

The nature of reason is to be active and focus on specifics. By comparison, intuition is general and effortless. Reason wants to "do" while intuition wants to "be." Both of these functions of mind must be employed, in meditation and in daily life, if full mental potential is to be used. In Transcendental Meditation, reason conducts the practice by employing the technique, but effortlessness is the method of this employment. The result is experience of the mantra in ever more expanded (intuitive or general) states until it vanishes into objectless consciousness. Reason maintains its state of doing, but ever more quietly until it becomes pure Being in the Transcendent.

Effortless doing, whether used knowingly or unknowingly, is the only approach that can take the imperfect mind to a state of perfection. It is the ability of the mind to solve the problem of the mind. *Effortless doing is the only completely evolutionary posture that can be assumed by undeveloped consciousness.* It is the door hidden in the wall that has been missed by those who have looked only for doing or only for being.

Effortless doing is the way to let go of control without opening ourselves to destruction: If we don't do anything to remedy our condition, we will be trampled under by our desires, but by holding on too tightly we block the impulses of desire that leads to our true nature. Effortless doing is the superrational alternative to these two undesirables, another term for mental balance, the "middle way" taught by Buddha.

Reason cannot regard effortless doing as a natural mode of the mind. Effort, or trying, seems more natural. Given this mental proclivity, particularly in the West, effortless doing is often turned into its exact opposite: trying to be. In trying to be, the mind contradicts itself: The effortless state of Being can never be achieved by the mental turbulence of trying.

Because the goal of meditation is silence, there is less need for "doing" the closer we approach it. And by of the laws of motion, the farther we go the faster we go.

The TM-Sidhi Program

In 1976 Maharishi introduced a series of advanced techniques called the TM-Sidhi program. The Sanskrit word *siddhi* comes from the roots *sid*, meaning "power", and *dhi*, "mind". The siddhis (Maharishi eliminated one of the d's to distinguish his program from past misuse of these practices) are supernormal powers—natural abilities of the human mind that have lain dormant for centuries. The purpose of this advanced program is to hasten development of higher states of consciousness and bestow mastery over Natural Law.

The TM-Sidhi techniques are practiced by use of the *sutras* (aphorisms) devised long ago by Maharishi Patanjali and written down as the *Yoga Sutras*. They come from Patanjali's cognitions of the capabilities of human consciousness at the subtlest level of thought. Many of the sutras allow extension of the senses into the cosmos for direct experience of what is going on there. *Patanjali's sutras* are pubic knowledge and can be found in the book *How to Know God* by Christopher Isherwood and Swami Prabhavananda. No instructions are provided however, and results cannot be produced without proper training.

The sense-expanding sutras are internal models from which society has structured external technologies. Among them are "seeing and hearing things far existing or hidden from view" (television and telephone), "knowledge of bodily systems" (x-rays and CAT-scans), "knowledge of the cosmic spaces and the motion and arrangement of the stars" (telescope), and "Yogic Flying" (airplane). Because Yogic Flying develops command over gravity—the most fundament law of Nature—it inculcates the daily-life ability to act in accord with all of Natural Law for maximum support of Nature in one's activities; thus it is called "the king of the siddhis." Other sutras are designed to expand compassion, friendliness, happiness and other human traits to the transcendental degree.

Knowledge of the motion of the stars is a good example

of what we mentioned in Chapter One—that when one is conscious at the subtlest level of the mind (where successful sutra practice takes place) he can be conscious anywhere in the cosmos. From the Transcendent, the vision opens to a view or experience on the basis of the intent carried by the specific sutra—in this case, what's going on with the stars. Former MUM philosophy professor Jonathan Shear was familiar with Plato's writing about the motion of the stars and had seen his diagram of this motion in the *Republic*. (See pages 195 and 196.) On one of Maharishi's early Sidhi's courses, Dr. Shear asked participants who had seen the motion of the stars to diagram it. Of fifty-three course participants, thirty-six submitted drawings. These corresponded significantly with Plato's diagrams of the umbrella-shaped circling of the heavenly bodies around the pole star. See diagrams on following pages:

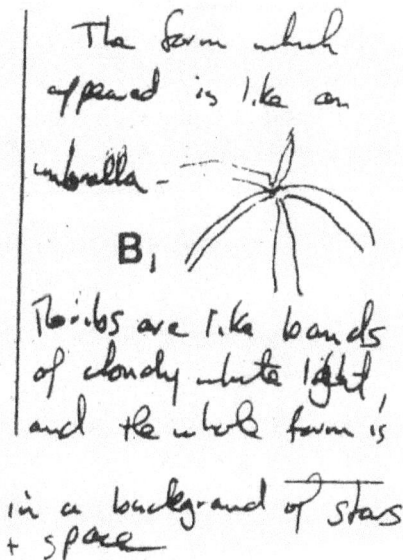

Course participants R.A. and R.S. describe their rough sketches as follow. B1: "The form which appeared is like an umbrella. The ribs are like bands of cloudy white light and the whole form is in a background of stars and space"....

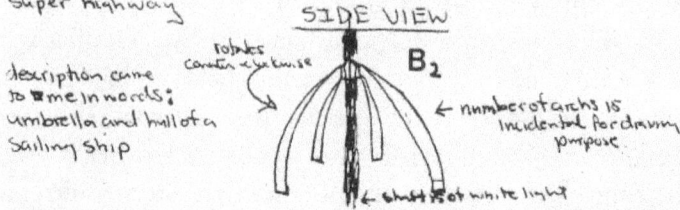

Pole Star: often I see :
a single bright star as if it's a shining gem to which other clumps of stars which look like archs of light or rainbows are attached. This whole arrangement rotates counter-clockwise at times slowly. Pole star has a wide shaft of blinding white light, brighter than any other arch going thru its center like a super highway

SIDE VIEW

rotates counter clockwise

B₂

description came to me in words: umbrella and hull of a sailing ship

← number of archs is incidental for drawing purpose

← shaft is of white light

Pole Star: "Often I see a single bright star as if it's a shining gem to which other clumps of stars, which look like arches of light or rainbows, are attached. This whole arrangement rotates counter-clockwise at times slowly. Pole Star has wide a shaft of blinding white light, brighter than any other arch, going through its center like a super highway...Description came to me in words: umbrella and hull of a sailing ship."

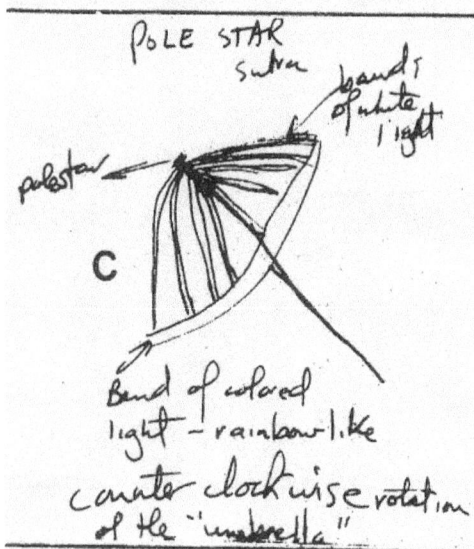

POLE STAR
Sutra

bands of white light

polestar ←

C

Band of colored light — rainbow-like

counter clockwise rotation of the "umbrella"

C: 'Bands of white light' is the description of the ribs extending downward from the "polestar" to the "Band of colored light—Rainbow-like counter-clockwise rotation of the umbrella."

These sketches and descriptions correspond with those in Plato's *Republic*.

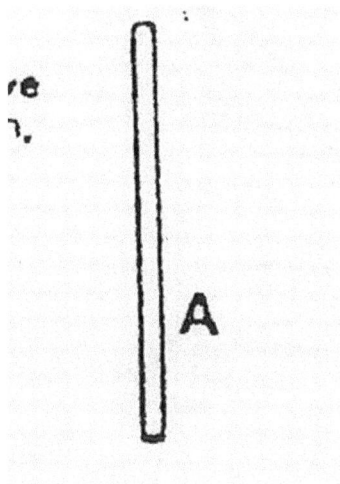

"They discerned extended from above throughout the heaven and the earth, a straight light like a pilar, most nearly resembling the rainbow, but brighter and purer…

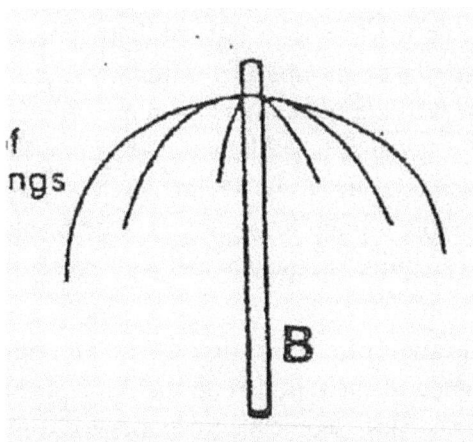

and they saw there at the middle of the light the extremities of the fastenings stretched from heaven, for this light was the girdle of the heavens...

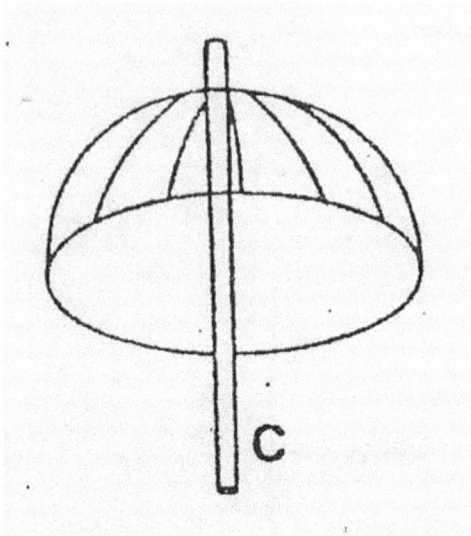

...holding together the entire revolving vault."

Shear's article, *Maharishi, Plato and the TM-Sidhi Program on Innate Structures of Consciousness* was published in *Metaphilosophy Magazine*, v. 12 # 1, January, 1981; it contains a summation of the above: "The pole-star is seen at the end of a long, rotating shaft of light. Rays of light come out from the shaft like the ribs of an umbrella. The umbrella-like structure on which the stars are embedded is seen rotating. Along the axis of light are other umbrella-like structures, one nested within the other, each rotating at its own rate, each with its own color, and each making a pure, lovely sound. The whole experience is described as quite spectacular, blissful, colorful and melodious."

The realization of a sutra; that is, the experience that the sutra is designed to elicit, occurs on the Principle of Desire and Transcendence. Most people have experienced this principle in daily life. We may desire, hope or pray for something for a long time without result, but when we forget about it (while still desiring it) it appears. This forgetting about it is analogous to taking a thought to the level of Being where it dissolves, assumes infinite power, and is thus immediately fulfilled. This was discussed at the beginning of Chapter Eight as the Principle of Full Intent. When thought is transcended while the flying sutra is being entertained, the thought vanishes and all that remains is the intent to fly that is inherent in attempting the sutra in the first place. From that intention raised to transcendental power, the body lifts up, moves forward and lands. From the first TM-Sidhi course in 1976 reports of experiences came to teachers in the field. Several of these reports, from different people, said that it seemed to be a sudden upsurge of joy that caused the body to lift up.

Flying has been known in the Western world for hundreds of years. Joseph of Copertino, an Italian saint of the seventeenth century, and several other Christian saints often had difficulty staying on the ground during the ecstasy of performing the Mass. The flights of St. Joseph are the most well documented in the history of the Church, more than seventy having been clearly verified. Fr. Angelo Pastrovicchi wrote in his book *Saint Joseph of Copertino*:

> On one occasion Joseph was present at the investment of several nuns in the church of St. Clare at Copertino. As soon as the choir intoned the antiphon, "Come, thou bride of Christ," he was seen to hurry from the corner in which he knelt towards the confessor of the convent…grasp him by the hand, lift him by supernatural power from the floor, and rapidly dance about with him in the air. It would lead too far to recount all the raptures and flights through the air while the saint was at Copertino; suffice it to say that, according to the acts of his beatification, more than seventy such flights were recorded, not counting those which occurred daily at Holy Mass and generally lasted two hours.…

During his first stay in Rome he went with the Father General to pay homage to the Pope, Urban VIII. While kissing the feet of the Pontiff the saint, filled with reverence for Jesus Christ in the person of His Vicegerent, was enraptured and raised aloft till the Father General's command brought him back to his senses. The Pope marveled much and said to the Father General that if Father Joseph were to die during his pontificate, he himself would bear witness to the occurrence.

St. Teresa was also a frequent flyer. According to the *Encyclopedia Britannica*,

> Saint Teresa of Avila was another well-known saint who reported levitating. She told of experiencing it during states of rapture. One eye-witness, Sister Anne of the Incarnation, said Saint Teresa levitated about a foot and a half off the ground for about an hour.
>
> Saint Teresa wrote of one of her experiences: 'It seemed to me, when I tried to make some resistance, as if a great force beneath my feet lifted me up.' She did not become unconscious, but saw herself being lifted up.

Yogic Flying was systematized by Maharishi Patanjali, probably in the second century B.C.E. Yogananda refered to it as "hopping like a frog" in his *Autobiography*. This first stage of accomplishment requires bodily exertion to complete the impulse to lift up. Currently, some sidhas at Maharishi University of Management are experiencing the second stage—"floating," in which muscle use is not involved. In large-group flying practice a few sidhas have been known to remain in the air for a moment or two and then lift higher before coming down.

John Hagelin, head of the physics department and Director of the Institute of Science, Technology and Public Policy at MUM has explained this phenomenon. Dr. Hagelin is one of the greatest physicists of our time. He has been a researcher at the European Center for Partical Physics (CERN) and at the Stanford Linear Accelerator (SLAC) and in 1992 was awarded the Kilby International Award for his work in partical physics leading to the development of supersymmetric grand unification theories. Dr. Hagelin explains Yogic Flying as based on the "reshaping of gravity" at the subtlest level of physicality. (Physicists have known for many years that gravity is not a force but a shape of space.) Dr. Hagelin says that one doesn't countermand or defy gravity but alters its direction and "falls upward." The natural power of gravity is reshaped by the supernatural power of intention at its transcendental source. To put it another way, the all-knowing Self created gravity; therefore it shouldn't be surprising if it can re-create it at its fundamental level. (All of this and much more is discussed in Craig Pearson's *Complete Book of Yogic Flying* published by MUM Press.)

When the thought of the flying sutra dissolves into the Transcendent, the subtle intention to fly stimulates the junction point between silence and dynamism. One is conscious of silence and dynamism simultaneously; at that moment he *is* silence and dynamism. This is an experience of Totality (Brahm)—the simultaneity of infinity and point we discussed in Chapter Two. Here is the spark that ignites the bonfire of bliss. Ecstasy is the same phenomenon whether it is a religious experience (causing Christian flyers to lift up) or a systematically produced psycho-physiological experience. In both cases, the highest universal power is brought into play.

One evening Maharishi was explaining Yogic Flying to a large group of meditators that included some of their children. At one point he said that instead of riding in a taxi we could zoom along in the air above it. One young boy stood up and said, "But Maharishi, if it was wintertime it would be too cold." Maharishi laughed and expressed delight in childrens' ability to see to the bottom of things. (Most adults, in our jadedness to overstated claims, discount what we could once see and thus block ourselves from seeing.) Maharishi then explained that when consciousness achieves the level of the Uncreated it is qualityless, and therefore the body doesn't feel dualities like cold and heat.

The purpose of the siddhis, and particularly Yogic Flying, is only in part the bliss we experience during the practice. It is to inculcate the ability to spontaneously accord our thought and action with the laws of Nature for bliss, meaning and achievement in daily life. In particular, Maharishi says, it is to hasten the realization of the sixth and seventh states of consciousness: God consciousness and unity consciousness.

We said in Chapter One ("The Holy of Holies") that God the Father, the Creator, resides at the subtlest level of physicality where universal manifestation begins. God consciousness, then, is the ability to perceive the world from that level. We said that the two highest states of consciousness develop after cosmic consciousness on the basis of growing love. Maharishi says that in God consciousness there is an expanded love of God and an enriched appreciation for things in general. In God consciousness, worldly objects are apt to be surrounded by a faint golden glow, or halo. One day while attending an Advanced Training Course at Cobb Mountain, California, I walked into the lecture room after a morning of long meditations and was early enough to get a seat on the front row. One of the course participants was in front of the room doing an impromptu stand-up routine and everyone was laughing. I had a feeling of lightness and happiness and then a powerful upwelling of love. Then to my amazement I saw him surrounded by a gold light as he continued to move around in front of the room laughing and joking.

Unity consciousness occurs when the subtlest relative perception (characteristic of God consciousness) rises to Absolute perception. But Maharishi refers to this as "cognition," since the word "perception" implies the senses. Absolute Being, the Self, that is now shining within and without the object of one's attention cannot, strictly speaking, be perceived (but only cognized) because it is transcendental, beyond the reach of the senses. On my Teacher Training Course Maharishi explained a second level of unity consciousness: Sometime after one is able to cognize the Absolute in the primary object of his attention, this recognition rises to include the entire universe at once. This he called Brahman consciousness—awareness of Totality. The experience of Atma as Brahm, discussed in the introduction, has been fully realized.

In the late 1970s, practitioners of the TM-Sidhi program began to gather at then-Maharishi International University for large-group practice of the program. Many of these people, for room and board and a small stipend, built the Maharishi Patanjali Golden Dome of Pure Knowledge on the campus to accommodate large groups of men. A similar dome was built for the ladies. MIU sociologists had a few years earlier discovered that when the percentage of a city's population that has been instructed in Transcendental Meditation reaches one percent, crime and other negative social behaviors decrease. This soon came to be called the Maharishi Effect. In the mid-1970's scientists at Maharishi International University computed that the square root of one percent of the world population practicing the Sidhi program in large groups would be enough to "reverse the trends of time" in the direction of all positivity in every area of life. This is now known as the Extended Maharishi Effect.

The Extended Maharishi Effect has been confirmed in studies done by Maharishi University of Management scientists as well as many independent researchers. One such researcher wrote that the MUM studies are on the leading edge of research into the possibility of a Unified Field. He said he didn't fully understand it, that few people do, but that the planning and execution of the studies was impeccable as, he believed, were the conclusions.

Research into Unified Field effects has been going on for many years. It has been shown that an event at one place in the universe (that is, in one part of the Unified Field) creates an affect in another part without the passage of time. (Maharishi said, "If you tickle it here, it laughs over there.") This phenomenon is explained in Bell's Theorem: If the spin of one particle of a pair of subatomic particles is reversed, the spin of the other particle, no matter how far removed, simultaneously reverses. The conclusion is that the Unified Field is the "everywhereness" of one thing.

In large-group practice of the TM-Sidhi program, a tidal wave of purity builds up that immediately effects the surrounding environment in ever-expanding waves. The synergistic power of 1500 to 2000 people is colossal, but even more important is the internal influence. Waves of positivity roll through the Unified Field of the Transcendent that connects everyone everywhere, enriching Earth's collective consciousness and bringing everything in creation to a higher level of evolution.

The world is currently living through the darkness before the dawn, but Maharishi said recently in reference to the on-going success of Yogic Flying, that "the weight that has been holding the Enlightened on the ground is being lifted from the shoulders of the world." When even one person breaks through the barrier of collective stress, either in meditation or the Sidhi practice, the breach remains opens for others. Maharishi's establishment of the Global Country of World Peace is a result of the progress that has been made in the last thirty-five years. The progress in Yogic flying has also resulted in the observed and subjectively testified fact that, again owing to deep movements in the Unified Field, new sidhas are having a level of experience equal to that of those who have been practicing for twenty or thirty years.

Maharishi is on record as having predicted the Extended Maharishi Effect soon after coming to America in the late 1950s. It is a principle known in the Vedas and is taught in Maharishi Vedic Science.

When the experience of the sidhas is combined with scientific research on the Extended Maharishi Effect, the door of the world is thrown open to the full sunshine of an Age of Enlightenment. In these explosive times, the holistic enrichment of global consciousness with peace, happiness, increased personal achievement, and feelings of security may well prove the Extended Maharishi Effect to be, as Maharishi has said, "the greatest discovery in the history of science."

In Unity consciousness one experiences his own consciousness as the sole constituent of all objects and events. He is eternally unified with the universe and all that's in it. We said at the beginning that the first sense of separation from our surroundings as infants will eventually close to a unified cognition of the world as nothing but Myself. This is it—the human birthright we will all realize—bliss ineffable, the life Divine. With all of his elaborate and sometimes hard-to-understand teachings throughout the world over the last fifty-four years of his life, Maharishi was still able to say, "The highest and sublest teaching remains: everything is going to be alright."

APPENDIX

Maharishi Consciousness-based Education

Consciousness-based education would be the study of academic disciplines on the basis of the continually expanding consciousness of the student, so that learning is easier and more enjoyable.

Maharishi's unique, revolutionary system is based on the understanding and demonstrable experience that all knowledge resides in human consciousness at the source of thought. This "home of all knowledge" as Maharishi has termed it, is not a new idea: The Latin *ex ducere*, from which our word "education" derives, means to lead forth or bring out. Dr. Jonathan Shear, in his article Maharishi, Plato and the TM-Sidhi Program on Innate Structures of Consciousness, discussed in Chapter 10 of the text, says, "According to Plato we are born with this [transcendental] knowledge in a latent, potential form; experience can activate these potentials; and it is the activation of these potentials which underlies all our subsequent knowledge."

What is new to this era is the activation factor of Maharishi's system—the scientifically verified technique of Transcendental Meditation®, by which the mind easily and systematically experiences the source of thought and thus opens itself to all-knowing consciousness. This expansion of consciousness concurrent with external learning is vital if education is to be complete. For lack of an effective procedure to bring this about, however, it has been ignored by modern education systems in favor of mere deposits of knowledge into a fixed container of consciousness.

Being the home of all knowledge, transcendental consciousness underlies all subsequent knowledge of existence as the Unified Field of Natural Law underlies all knowledge of the physical universe. The Unified Field is a Western scientific term for the transcendental consciousness long known in the Vedic science of the East. As the creative level of the physical universe and therefore of the human organism, this unbounded, eternal field of existence is often referred to as the Self. Indeed, one may experience it as himself when thought is transcended.

Therefore, when one studies physics at Maharishi University of Management facilities throughout the world, he is studying the Unified Field of existence as his own Self. Likewise in mathematics. The abstract, unbounded null set [0], which is the mathematical equivalent of the unbounded Self, is the source of all the numbers and therefore of all of mathematics. The same is true in literature and the other arts, where the inspirational muse corresponds to the deepest level. History becomes his-story. In Maharishi's system of education, all academic subjects are regarded as aspects of the one over-arching subject that is the student's own Self. Thus, education is a joyous process—as joyous and meaningful as oneself is to oneself.

The thirst for knowledge is man's most compelling impulse. When what is being learned is oneself, this innate drive is raised to its highest power. After a visit of the North Central Association of the Higher Learning Commission to the M.U.M. campus in Fairfield, Iowa, one official remarked that it was the only educational institution he had seen where students entered and left the classroom discussing the subject matter.

As the student progresses, there is a growing correspondence between inner and outer knowledge. Through both the "laboratory work" of Transcendental Meditation and in the classroom lectures, where the academic subjects are regarded as aspects of the Self, the Self increasingly comes to be known to be the source and the goal of all knowledge.

Over 600 scientific research studies have been conducted on the Transcendental Meditation and TM-Sidhi programs at more that 200 universities and research institutions in 30 countries, and published in over 125 scientific journals. These papers have been reprinted in *Scientific Research on Maharishi's Transcendental Meditation and TM-Sidhi Programme: Collected Papers, Volumes 1-6*. Some of the studies relevant here are as follow.

Optimization of Brain Functioning. (*International Journal of Neuroscience*, numbers 13 and 15). "Higher levels of EEG coherence measured during the practice of the Transcendenal Meditation technique are significantly correlated with increased fluency of verbal creativity, increased efficiency in learning new concepts; more principled moral reasoning, higher verbal IQ and decreased neuroticism, higher academic achievement, and increased neurological efficiency as measured by faster recovery of the paired H-reflex." Increased Self-Actualization. (*Journal of Social Behavior and Personality and Journal of Counseling Psychology*). "Statistical meta-analysis of all available studies (42 independent outcomes) indicate that the effect of the Transcendal Meditation program on increasing self-actualization is much greater than in concentration, contemplation, or other techniques. Self-actualization refers to realizing more of one's inner potential, expressed in every area of life: integration and stability of personality, self-regard, emotional maturity, capacity for warm interpersonal relationships, and adaptive response to challenges." Reduced Anxiety. A statistical meta-analysis conducted at Stanford University of all available studies (142 independent outcomes) and published in the *Journal of Clinical Psychology* indicated that "the effect of the Transcendental Meditation program on reducing trait anxiety was much greater than that of concentration or contemplation or other techniques. Analysis showed that these positive results conld not be attributed to subject expectation, experimenter bias, or quality of research design."

The consciousness-based system is designed to meet all the needs of the human organism. The universe is structured by Natural Laws expressing themselves from the transcendental level. Therefore the student makes increasingly greater use of what Maharishi refers to as the Home of All the Laws of Nature. Thinking and acting increasingly in accord with Natural Law in all his activities, the student draws all achievement and happiness to himself.

It is the common experience in traditional education that as knowledge grows, the field of the unknown expands correspondingly. Thus, the happiness that is the natural result of knowledge is accompanied by growing frustration and doubt. But this is only in part because we have become aware of how much more there is to learn.

We are also handicapped by using only five to 10 percent of our mental potential so that the areas of the brain that take part in perception are quite limited. But the Transcendental Meditation technique frees the brain's latent abilities. A paper titled <u>Mobilization of the Latent Reserves of the Brain</u> (published in *Human Physiology* and presented at the *International Symposium "Consciousness and the Brain" of the Russian Academy of Science*) found that "during the Transcendental Meditation program...the brain's response to somatosensory stimulation [is] more widely distributed across the cortex." This study, by Dr. Nicolai Nicolaevich Lyubimov, Director of the Moscow Brain Research Institute's Laboratory of Neurocybernetics, indicates that "during the Transcendental Meditation program there is an increase in the areas of the cortex taking part in perception of specific information and an increase in the functional relationship beween the two hemispheres."

Large areas of the brain become ossified by partial use.

Over time we become more and more habituated to using only a small fraction of our mental potential, and thus it is more difficult to expand brain usage as time goes on. The Lyubimov study and others like it suggest, as Maharishi has said, that traditional education actually damages the brain. The human brain, with its incredibly diverse abilities, was obviously given us to be used in full. Therefore, an educational approach that repeatedly stimulates only isolated areas of the brain while ignoring the others leaves broader knowledge not only unknown but unknowable.

Considering the rapid expansion of knowledge today it shouldn't be surprising that we have found an organic way to rectify the functioning of the human brain.

Holistic expansion of brain functioning through Transcendental Meditation delivers to the student what Maharishi calls the Fruit of all Knowledge. Knowledge leads to happiness; we could think of them as two sides of the same coin. (Since Maharishi often talks about bliss, someone asked him what it feels like. He said, "Bliss feels like knowing something.") However, there is a point at which bliss and knowledge separate. As the acquirement of knowledge begins to be based on infusion of transcendental consciousness into the thinking mind, a sense of happiness begins to replace the former frustration with what we don't know. And with the permanent establishment of transcendental consciousness in the relative mind (called cosmic consciousness), ordinary happiness rises to a lasting state of bliss. This is the Fruit of all Knowledge: We experience happiness at its absolute level while our relative knowledge remains incomplete. We enjoy the fruit of a tree without owning the tree. Plus, with the progressive unfoldment of the brain's latent capabilities, what one doesn't know becomes increasingly knowable. Only at this point is one fully educated.

Maharishi University of Management has an open admissions policy—policy—almost everyone with a high school diploma is admitted. There is no SAT or entrance-tests requirement. Owing to government students loans, many people have gotten an education through the doctorate level without paying out of pocket. More than 95% of the University's students receive financial aid. The typical award for U.S. students covers 90-100% of the tuition and fees.

A national study, sponsored by the Carnegie Foundation for the Advancement of Teaching, put the univeristy in the top 3% of U.S. colleges for "active and collaborative learning" and in the top 4% in "enriching educational experiences."

A national alumni survey by American College Testing (ACT) found that the percentage of the University's graduates answering "definitely yes" to the question "Would you choose this college again?" was 128% higher than the national norm for over 1,000 participating U.S. colleges and universities.

The University's graduates have been hired by thousands of companies and organizations in the U.S. and around the world, including many Fortune 500 companies. Many alumni have started their own businessess. (A former Governor of Iowa called Fairfield "the entrepreneurial capital of the state.") Graduates have been accepted at hundreds of graduate schools, including Harvard, Yale, Stanford, Duke, and Oxford.

The National Institutes of Health has awarded the University more than $20 million for research in natural medicine.

The University's professors have higher degrees from America's most distinguished universities, including Harvard, MIT, Stanford, Yale, Johns Hopkins, Notre Dame, Purdue, and the Univeristy of Michigan. Students learn from top professors—not graduate students—in small classes starting from the first year. Undergraduate and graduate degrees are offered in the arts, sciences, business, and the humanities.

The M.U.M. campus and the city of Fairfield are Iowa's center for sustainable living. The University offers a popular undergraduate program in this subject. Jefferson county has the most acreage of organic crops of any county in Iowa, and Fairfield has become a national model for green development, primarily for its state-of-the-art EgoVillage. The city hosts an EcoFair each Spring.

With students from throughout the U.S. and more than 60 foreign countries, representing many cultures and every major religion, the University is located on 272 acres of rolling farmland. Fairfield is a cosmopolitan city of 10,000 people fifty miles west of the Mississippi River. It is the creative arts center of Southeast Iowa with an exceptionally lively theatre and music scene, and 25 art galleries around the town square.

Students learn research-proven methods for creating and maintaining a balanced state of health. These techniques enliven the inner intelligence of the body and strengthen its natural healing ability. The University serves freshly prepared organic vegetarian meals, using locally grown produce.

Students who are not already practicing Transcendental Meditation learn the technique at the time of enrollment. The one-year Master's program in Maharishi Vedic Science can be entered by anyone with a Bachelor's degree. Maharishi Vedic Science is an almalgum of Maharishi's teachings ranging from awakening to Enlightenment, and is a complete spiritual education in itself. The current cirriculum is made up of the following courses:

Physiology, Consciousness and the Veda. Awaken your total brain potential.

Bhagavad-Gita Chapters 1-3. The principle of dharma, the eternal nature of life, and the effortlessness of transcending as the basis of right action.

Bhagavad-Gita Chapters 4-6. The roles of silence and action, knowledge and experience, in rising to higher states of consciousness.

Science of Being and Art of Living. Maharishi's guide to life in Enlightenment.

Principles of Maharishi Vedic Science. The self-referral dynamics of consciousness.

Advanced Study in Maharishi Vedic Science. Analyzing the fabric of immortality.

Sanskrit. Learning to read the Vedic literature to enliven the language of nature within.

Physics of Invincibility. The self-referral dynamics of the constitution of the universe and its unfoldment as glimpsed by contemporary unified quantum field theory.

Developing Brahman Consciousenss. Growing toward the supreme pinnacle of human evolution—all experience unified in the self.

Creating World Peace. Averting the birth of an enemy.

Practicum in Maharishi Vedic Technologies. Bringing health and wholeness to the community.

Synthesizing the Key Principles from Your Courses. In this course you will identify the key principles from all the courses in your graduate program, place them into the larger framework of your experience, and indicate how they can be applied to your daily life. This course enables you to summarize the knowledge and experience you have gained from the program.

All courses at M.U.M. are taught in one-month blocks. Attention is focused on one course at a time, minimizing evening homework. An exception to the block system is *Research into Consciousness.* This runs concurrently with all the other courses and consists of morning and evening campus-wide group practice of Transcendental Meditation and the TM-Sidhi program to develop a maximum state of rest.

Informative and enjoyable Visitors' Weekends are held on a regular basis.

The University is accredited by The Higher Learning Commission (www.ncahigherlearningcommission.org). For more information about Maharishi University of Management and Transcendental Meditation® contact the website www.mum.edu.

The consciousness-based curriculum of the Maharishi School of the Age of Enlightenment (grades K-12), located on the M.U.M. campus in Fairfield, systematically develops the full potential of every student and teacher through twice-daily practice of the Transcendental Meditation technique. The Upper School (grades 10-12) consistently scores in the 99th percentile on standardized national tests of academic achievement. This result is particularly notable in light of the fact that when first admitted to the school, the students as a whole score at around the fiftieth percentile. No other school in the United States produces this great a change in its student body as a whole. Over the past many years, an average of 95% of graduates of the Maharishi School have continued with higher education, attending four-year colleges and universities. Over the past several years, 5% of Maharishi School seniors have been named National Merit Scholar Finalists. This is about ten times greater than the national norm.

Educators are becoming increasingly aware that schools must structure both inner and outer student development. The on-going and worsening outbreaks of violence in schools, the continuing epidemic of substance abuse, and the shocking rise in student stress indicate that current educational approaches are not satisfying the inner needs of our children.

Maharishi School of the Age of Enlightenment has implemented practical, well-rounded education programs for the last 31 years. These programs devote time and attention to students' outer performance as well as to the inner quality of their lives. Students have won first-place state titles in science, speech, drama, writing, art, history, mathematics, chess, tennis, golf, spelling, Odyssey of the Mind, and Destination ImagiNation (international, creative, problem-solving competitions). Upper School grades regularly score in the 99th percentile on the Iowa Tests of Educational Development although the school maintains an open admissions policy. The school has produced 29

National Merit Scholar Finalists. Research published in *Educa-tion* journal shows significant increases in acadmic achievement for transfer students after only one year at the School.

Student achievement results in part from an exceptional learning environment. In addition to direct instruction, students learn through hands-on experiments, guest speakers, projects, field trips, research, videos, demonstrations, workshops, whole and small group discussion, manipulatives, inquiry-based activities, interdisciplinary study, computer software, and team problem-solving.

Jill Olsen-Virlee, a recent Iowa Teacher of the Year, said after a visit, "Your school was truly an inspiration. The inner peace, the concern for one another, the respect and thirst for wisdom, and a holistic approach to the children are awesome." Julia Herbert, Ed.S., of the Washington, D.C. area schools said, "As a reading consultant I have visited many public and private schools, and I have never felt such a calm and silent atmosphere in a school of bright, lively, alert children as was evident at Maharishi School of the Age of Enlightenment."

A few years ago, a delegation of Iowa educators toured the School. One educator, amazed by what he saw and by the School's achievements, asked one of the teachers, "Where do you get these kids?" The teacher smiled and said, "We make them here."

The school welcomes visitors (particularly, parents of prospective strudents) to observe first-hand the process and results of consciousness-based education. In 2010 a delegation of educators from China visited the School. To make an appointment to visit the School, contact the Registrar at 641/472-9400 or Registrar@msae.edu.

The website of Maharishi School of the Age of Enlightenment is www.maharishischooliowa.org.

www.ingramcontent.com/pod-product-compliance
Lightning Source LLC
Chambersburg PA
CBHW020451100426
42813CB00031B/3329/J